FRANÇOIS MAURIAC was born at Bordeaux, France, in 1885 and educated in that city at Roman Catholic schools and at Bordeaux University. "The history of Bordeaux," he says, "is the history of my body and my soul: it is my childhood and my youth crystallized."

Mauriac undertook philosophical studies at the Ecole des Chartes in Paris, but gradually abandoned scholarship for the writing of fiction. *A Kiss for the Leper,* a novel written in 1922, quickly made him famous; and his writings since that time have won him world renown. In 1933 he was elected a member of the French Academy. Shortly afterward he began his controversial writings which he continued during the years of resistance under the name of Forez, and in 1945 became a brilliant leader-writer on *Le Figaro.* In 1952, M. Mauriac won the Nobel Prize: a fitting recognition of the original type of novel he has evolved and of his many admirable plays. In 1959, Mauriac was elected an honorary member of the American Academy of Arts and Letters.

THE WORLD PUBLISHING COMPANY • CLEVELAND AND NEW YORK

1931

# THE SON OF MAN

# The Son of Man

*by*
FRANÇOIS MAURIAC

*Translated by*
BERNARD MURCHLAND

THE WORLD PUBLISHING COMPANY

CLEVELAND AND NEW YORK

*Published by* The World Publishing Company
2231 West 110th Street, Cleveland 2, Ohio

*Published simultaneously in Canada by*
Nelson, Foster & Scott Ltd.

First published in Paris by Bernard Grasset, Editeur
under the title *Le Fils de l'homme*.

Library of Congress Catalog Card Number: 60-5803

FIRST EDITION

© 1958 by Éditions Bernard Grasset.

Nihil obstat

MYLES M. BOURKE, S.T.D.
CENSOR LIBRORUM

Imprimatur

✠ FRANCIS CARDINAL SPELLMAN
ARCHBISHOP OF NEW YORK

September 21, 1959

The nihil obstat and imprimatur are official declarations that a book or pamphlet is free of doctrinal or moral error. No implication is contained therein that those who have granted the nihil obstat and imprimatur agree with the contents, opinions or statements expressed.

To

*Elie Wiesel*

who was a crucified Jewish child.

His friend

F.M.

# Contents

# Translator's Preface

THERE is an intense and incomplete quality in Mauriac's writing: a quality more characteristic of poetry than of prose. In translating this book I was constantly reminded of his genius for compressing deep thought in seductively simple, fragmentary language—as if he were compelled to catch a fleeting insight on the wing. It may also be said that Mauriac's heart speaks more than his pen; his vision is, as it were, always one step beyond the potential of linguistic expression. Mauriac is, moreover, disturbingly apocalyptic; the reader feels that he is employing his artistic talent as a bulwark against some imminent disaster.

For all these reasons I felt obliged to translate Mauriac's prose in terms of his vision. Every effort was, of course, made to remain faithful to the subtlety of his prose. In some instances, however, literal translation was not possible; and in such cases, a suitable English idiom was substituted. Wherever this was necessary I became painfully aware of the succinct, penetrating nature of the French and of the power in Mauriac's book.

It is indeed a powerful book. Much of it ranks with anything the French Academician has ever written for its depth and high sense of awareness. If, as Mauriac said in a recent interview, he is a "master of uneasiness," he seems in a pre-eminent way to be uneasy about matters of consequence. He is uneasy, for example, about man's cruelty to man and the seemingly perennial inability of the Christian to honor his most basic commitments—commitments that can be summarized in one shattering word: love. Critics of Christianity who are, for one reason or another, outside the fold can argue embarrassingly to this point. But Mauriac would appear to be one critic within the fold who can smash false idols with prophetic wrath.

Mauriac is not, however, an angry man; nor is he a despairing man. Quite the contrary. He has frequently confessed his discouragement with what he calls the "frog pond" of current events and the present state of the Christian Church. But they are wrong who see in his discouragement or in his uneasiness a kind of despair. The very heart of Mauriac's vision—and this book proves it perhaps better than any other—is an awareness of the overpowering reality of love, the presence of God among men, man's eventual ability to transcend his limitations through the aid of grace. Mauriac defines the Christian as a sinner who is certain that hope prevails against despair and love against hatred. It is this certitude which, in Mauriac's view, delivers the Christian man up to the anguish of the Cross and makes him the glorious, tortured, and love-deserving creature he is.

Against the torn background of human torment, Mauriac unfolds the glory and the dignity of man. Against the unreality that pervades everything man touches, Mauriac establishes the reality of God. This is the vigorous dialectic that, in my view, makes *The Son of Man* a vibrant and challenging book.

BERNARD MURCHLAND

*Notre Dame*
*Summer 1959*

# THE SON OF MAN

*Striving for love all our lives, we never achieve
it except in so imperfect a manner that our hearts
bleed. But even if, while living, we were to achieve
it, what would remain of it after death? After our
death the prayers of our loved ones would follow
us into the next world, a pious memory would
still pronounce our name; but soon heaven and
earth move a step forward, oblivion falls upon us,
silence covers us, love's ethereal breeze no longer
ripples over our tomb. It is finished; it is forever
finished. Such is the history of man in search of
love.*

*But I am mistaken! For there is one man whose
tomb love still guards; there is one man whose
sepulcher is not only glorious, as the prophet says,
but whose sepulcher is loved. There is one man
whose ashes have not cooled after nineteen centuries and who is born anew each day in the
thoughts of a multitude of men. There is one man
who is dead and buried but whose sleep and awak-*

15

*ening is closely watched and whose words still vibrate with life, giving birth not only to love but also to virtue fructifying in love. This man has been attached to a cross for centuries; but each day thousands of people who adore him take him down from his throne of suffering: they kneel before him, they prostrate themselves as low as they can before him, they kiss his bleeding feet with inexpressible ardor.*

*This man was scourged, crucified, and killed; but an unspeakable love resurrected him from death and from infamy; it placed him in the glory of a love that never weakens and that finds in him peace, honor, and joy even to the point of ecstasy. This man was pursued by an inextinguishable hatred in his suffering and in his tomb; but he asked for apostles and for martyrs to his name in every generation, and there has been no age without them. This man is the only human being ever to have founded a kingdom of love on the earth; and this man is You, O Jesus Christ!*

LACORDAIRE

# I

# The Mystery of Childhood

EVEN in our old age we have much in common with the little child in the crib; we recognize ourselves in that child and in a sense we are that child. One part of our being, a most hidden part, is the child who has not experienced evil; by this fact a part of our being is like unto God. For God is not only a Father; He is also an Eternal Child. I say this not because I adore the weakness and helplessness of the child. On the contrary, it is the child's strength which enraptures me: his all-powerfulness. Over the cadavers of Nietzschean heroes and the slaughterhouses which they filled with martyrs before adding to them the corruption of their own bodies, the purity of the child stands firm and triumphs.

Even in our own lives, no matter what they might have been, it is possible to discover that triumphant purity and to reawaken it.

After Communion a Christian enters within himself, crosses the thick layers of irreparable acts that coat his conscience, the heavy accumulation of forgiven sins. When I do this, I discover the child who returned to his place in the left pew, on the twelfth of May, 1896, in the chapel of a school that no longer exists. I am still that child; nothing has changed except that my body is already half destroyed. *But You are always there; You are there as the love I have seen reflected in the faces of the saints I have encountered during my life, the love to Whom I so often said: "Depart from me!"*

Today I know what Scripture means by "man of blood." I have seen men of blood. I will not be ashamed of my childhood before them. I put myself on the side of childhood—on the side of the assassinated child Abel as well as on the side of the victorious child David; of the child Joseph who reigned in Egypt and of the Hebrew children who sang their joy in a furnace and were subjected to lions and flames. I am, above all, on the side of the Infant God who promised happiness to the meek. In the eyes of the world the strong man is the brute propelled by the power of his instincts to those extremes—the mere sight of which is in itself a defilement!—that my generation has seen in Spain, in Germany, in Russia, and even, unfortunately, in my own country. After proclaiming the death of God by the mouth of Nietzsche, humanity sank into infamy, into an unspeakably foul cowardice which has culminated in the desperate zeal of executioners and police forces against unarmed and defenseless people.

But the Infant God naked upon the straw is the only one who is really all-powerful. He has within His fragile being the double torrent of two natures: "The Word was made flesh." By analogy, and infinitely distant from this mystery of mysteries, carnal and sinful man is united to the incarnate love of this Child through the grace he received upon his entry into this world. I, too, possess an eternal childhood and a sinful flesh; but I cannot bring them into harmony; one rises up over the other and each in its turn leads to death. *This tide of flesh and blood, O*

*God, this ebb and flow which both covers and uncovers my childhood, and the spume which seems to bury my childhood forever (although suddenly it is once more intact and I am like the little boy who wept in his pew on May 12, 1896)—how can this tidal pull of human nature ever be brought into submission to You?*

*How difficult it is to keep my attention fixed on Your childhood, not to be drawn toward the abyss of your tortured humanity, toward Your passion and Your death. I am attracted to Your passion by our resemblance in suffering; because suffering summed up and, as it were, defined Your humanity, an instinct precipitates those who love You to the call of Your halting voice, toward the moments of agony and suffering in Your life. But it is not at the foot of the Cross that we are closest to You; it is perhaps while kneeling before Your manger, before the God-Child who has just been born. O Infinite Child, we do not expect You to forgive us for crimes which You do not yet understand.*

*What attracted me to Your adult body—tortured, crucified, and pierced with a lance—was its conformity to mine. O sorrowful Christ, in whom I seek myself and in whom I find myself, give me the grace to stop by Your manger, to lean at length over Your Infinite Being totally captured within a little flesh.* The sentiment of adoration which overcomes me when I hold the infant in my arms in no way resembles the bitter happiness I experience when I remember the Cross upon which is nailed a body like mine. For in the manger is Him whom we call God (but that is not His real name) and who is not yet called Jesus. He will receive the name of Jesus later in His life, although, in another and very real sense He undoubtedly received this name from all eternity. But upon the straw of Bethlehem He is still "He who is"; not the Child-God but the God Who has become a Child: the God-Child, a child who is like a river uncontaminated by human sinfulness.

Trembling with joy, kneeling over the common graves of Europe and carrying within me the memories of concentration camps, the charred cadavers of children and women in the ruins of French, German, Russian, and Japanese cities, I adore Him. *I believe in you, God-Child, because you are a love that is still blind, that is still ignorant of innumerable crimes.* To know them would in some way be to participate in them; but the Child of the manger is a stranger to this spilled blood, He is ignorant of the human stain. He will later see all of this before expiating it. But the Child of the manger knows nothing of it at this time. He still radiates infinite innocence. God in Him, omniscient God, has as yet undergone nothing, experienced nothing.

He is of course eternal knowledge; in a few years He will experience the suffering of mankind along the roads to Galilee and Calvary. But meanwhile, the newborn in Bethlehem is innocence ignorant of itself, love which does not know itself, fire which is not aware that it is fire. Or perhaps He is aware? In any event, it is not what He knows about the human condition that attracts us; it is rather what He brings with Him from a kingdom that is not of this world.

All other children of men are born out of nothingness. This one emanates from Being, passes from eternity to time, from the eternal to the ephemeral. I turn for a brief instant from the face that bears the insults of our crimes to press the newborn close to my heart. On this Christmas night, I will not speak of my sins to Him; I will lull Him to sleep in my love as I would my first-born son. I cannot speak of evil to the incarnate ignorance of evil.

The open door through which, on the paternal side, a torrent of heredities submerges us, opens for this child upon infinite Being: upon the Father. From this source He inherits an ocean of divinity while we sinners reap the hidden passions of the dead of our race: a sinister torchlight procession in which each man leaves after him the torches that will consume his descendants and whose flames will end by setting fire to a world vowed to murder and to abominable vices. *O Lord who has escaped this heritage under which we groan and weep, who not only knows the secret of hearts but also those of the body, whom grace draws less toward the bad will of those who love You than toward the dark germs deposited by our ancestors, toward the "thorn in the flesh" that tortured Saint Paul, have mercy upon the madness of those who sometimes awaken in an abyss into which they fell long before their birth.*

*I will become a child to be near you, O God-Child. There is neither death nor old age for those who love You; otherwise how would they be saved?* For if it is true that the Lord asks those who follow Him to carry their cross, He does not enjoin them, except for a small number of saints, to be crucified as He was; on the other hand, He declares to all, whoever they might be, that they must become as little children to enter the kingdom and that they must receive the kingdom of God with the heart of a child. "Unless you become as one of these little ones . . ."

There is therefore no other means of salvation than to become like a child. How easy it is for an old author, bitter and cynical as he is, to accept this condition! *No one but you, O God, could believe it; You know it. My burning brow seeks You as a child seeks its mother's embrace: as a refuge, a shelter far from life's atrocities! You were as involved as anyone else in this life; yet You detected the child in everyone. Therefore those who seem ferocious to me undoubtedly carry within them this same child.*

Human ferocity is like an encrustation formed

by the alluvium of life; but the mystery of childhood remains at the center of being. True, our
childhood has been wounded by original sin; this
is why Freud is partly right. But I believe none
the less in the sanctity of childhood, in that good
faith, in that hope, in that sacred weakness
which we will conceal until our last breath.
This is the angelic part of human nature which
is called to see the Resurrection, to eternal contemplation of the Divine Face. *The world accused You of having calumniated life and of
creating an unfit and sickly race; yet, as You
raised Lazarus from the dead, so You raised up
beyond our infamous daily mediocrity a child:
an eternal child.*

Men always amuse themselves like children.
If, sitting in the shadows of my loge in the
theater, I turn my back on the actors who are
interpreting my play, I notice rows of attentive
or tired heads. I am always struck by how much
they resemble the public before the Punch-and-
Judy shows of my childhood. They have not
changed; they laugh or weep with their whole
hearts. In Alsace I saw the military leaders treat-
ing themselves to a parade every day of the

week; they found a source of inexhaustible joy in playing (as children they played with lead soldiers) with soldiers of flesh under a leaden sun. Men will, it seems, distract themselves with marbles and balls until the very end of life. Today they have real horses and real weapons. They no longer have to imagine, to invent, to re-create the real: this is a real horse which they feel between their legs and the gun in their hands kills "for real." Their crimes are also like those of a child: the Nazis, for example, pulled off the legs of human insects! The child's profound insensitivity to the suffering of animals betrays itself in the horror of what we have seen during these bloody years.

But if the corruption of childhood is the worst kind, then the sanctity of childhood is what most resembles God. This is what must be redeemed in every human being. Absolution revives it in most men only a little before death; it awakens innocence in the last tear on the cheek of a dying man. *Blessed is he, O Lord, who does not call you He who damns, as you remarked in a vision to my patron, Francis de*

*Sales, but who calls you Jesus, He who saves.*
And when the unspeakably foul wave of sinful
nature covers us, according to the ineluctable
laws of the tides (what ominous star regulates
the rise and fall of this filth in us?), there is no
explanation or excuse to be given to the infant
God: as a child, He would not understand.

We cannot hold this Child responsible for
the incomprehensible creation which He came
to save but which, since hell-fire will continue
throughout eternity, He did not save completely.
Though Infinite, He has been swallowed up in
a finite that is pockmarked with crimes. He
establishes His claim in this world with two
crossed pieces of wood; yet in the name of that
cross, millions of martyrs and executioners have
been raised up, people have been burned at the
stake, crusades and wars have been unleashed,
and human beings have been dominated by inhuman laws. The gentle child shivers with cold
on the edge of a criminal world while angels
promise peace to men of good will—a peace
that can be discovered only after a full measure
of suffering; but in the shadows of His birth-

place Herod's soldiers sharpen their knives for a slaughter of innocents that will apparently never end.

This is the Christian paradox; these are the parts of an undecipherable mystery to which the Child has the secret word. When He became a man, He did not tell us what that word is; still, we know that it exists. Christ implied as much when His disciples murmured: "But will no one be saved?" And He answered: "Man can do nothing; but all things are possible to God." This last secret word will not be given to us until our malice can no longer use it as an excuse for satisfaction of our vices. Until the end of time the little child will keep the secret, which man would use only to glut himself. A nature or a definition of God does not exist; but there is a Love Which Knows Itself and which is reflected in creatures mysteriously wounded from their birth.

This wound is envenomed and irritated by that somber angel who is master of the world; the world, however, no longer even believes that Satan exists. Penetrated as it is with an essential malignancy, history is more determined than

28

modern man realizes. And there is no one to disturb this maleficent order except the Infant God. *Sometimes I wanted to withdraw from You. I could no longer bear Your silence, Your absence. For what can be more absent than a newborn child? With whom is one more alone than with a little child in his arms? To accept the risk of our unimaginable anger, to mingle with the crowd of those who believe only in man on earth, in his strength, in his body (whose flesh is gorged with riches and full of hidden powers), who do not try to be either good or pure—at certain moments, I desired all these things.* But it was not permitted to me to have them since I have been branded from childhood. *"You are simply a product of influences of your childhood,"* my demon mockingly whispered. *"Until your last breath,"* he seemed to say, *"you will feed in this false and empty pasture."* Sometimes, in my hours of grace, I believed I had lost this demon in the crowd behind me. I no longer felt his breath on my neck. Then I knew what the saints experienced; I caught a glimpse of their life, and already I was stripping myself on the edge of an ocean of life. The peace of

Christ intoxicated me. How did I ever consent to live without this joy? How simple death would be if it were a passage from ecstasy to contemplation, from the desire of God to the possession of God!

But then my peace would be shattered. A vague sadness would overcome me, a desire to be walking the streets, to look into the cold, impassioned face of a prostitute; there would be a contempt for my life, for what I have been, for what I am, a hatred for my destiny. How I desired to blur those images and to disappear: to leave of myself nothing but a castoff garment, to forget my name and my age in a world which does not reflect God or give me any reminder of Him. *Infant God, you know that we do not love peace; we do not love happiness. The emptiness of heart, the eternal vacuity of incipient old age, the insipidity of the idle days which You give us, the residue of a life which stagnates in academies and in official places—how all of this gives savor to the bitterness of dead passions!*

*Not that I was ever very far away from Your manger; but it was unnecessary even to leave it at all. There was no need for a single thing, or even the shadow of a thing, to come between us and to prevent me from seeing You, O Child, above all creatures! The saints have overcome the obstacles of flesh and blood, have gone beyond the limits of sinful nature. But how many Christians have failed to do so? Who will ever know? The saints have gone beyond earthly barriers to the place where You are supposed to await them; sometimes You are not there or at least seem not to be there. And sometimes, hidden, You watch the disappointment of those who, at the price of their poor human happiness, hastened to the rendezvous You assigned them: You see that they seek You but do not find You; yet they believe; they know that You are there. How can they turn back? They can only go forward into the desert of Your divinity. What is important for them is not to grow weary but to possess a heart that will not fail. The callousness and insensitivity of an old man are what remain in him after the ebb and flow of love has failed to reach its object; but he discovers this object, this being, this love, on the Blessed Night of Christmas. He recognizes it; he presses it against his breast like a sleeping child.*

The Eucharist is the childhood of God; it is in me as a little child who falls asleep and whose head rests lightly on my shoulders. But it is an ardent sleep, a presence that both burns and pacifies. I bear it away with me hidden, as it were, under my cloak. God has not answered my questions laden with despair: He has simply given Himself to me.

# I I

# The Hidden Life

IT IS very confusing to recall that, for a period of thirty years, the Son of God did not appear to be anything other than a man. What is particularly astonishing in this regard is not the miracles of His public life, but the absence of miracles during His hidden life. If everything Luke writes concerning the Virgin—the annunciation of the angel, Mary's visit to her cousin Elizabeth, whose soul leaped for joy in the presence of God her savior—is simply a myth; if the report about the shepherds is also mythical—that, on that night of nights, under the stars as well as in their hearts, they received the promise of "peace to men of good will," a promise which still nourishes our hope after

nineteen centuries; and if, finally, it was a cred-
ulous love that wove this legend about the crib
of the Child—a legend that supposedly became
true to the degree that Jesus was considered
God—if all these things are so, then why was
the web of imaginings interrupted after the first
moments of childhood? Why didn't it apply to
Christ as a little boy, as an adolescent, or as a
young man?

Even today the old man Simeon stands on the
threshold of the hidden life; he presses the child
against his breast; he sees nations dazzled by the
light which, for a brief moment, he holds in
his hands. He sees the sword that will pierce
the heart of Mary and he prophesies it. But then
it seems a curtain is drawn; a shadow covers the
child about whom Luke reports nothing further,
except the episode of the flight into Egypt and
the finding of Jesus in the temple where He
astonished the doctors of the law. This latter
point, certainly, is enough to make us understand
what kind of Jewish child He was; such children
still exist, as is shown by what I have recently
read in *La Nuit*, the diary of Elie Wiesel who
was deported to Germany when he was a little

boy and barely escaped the furnaces where his family and relatives were burned to death. "When I was a boy, my faith was very strong," he wrote. "During the day I would study the *Talmud* and at night I would go to the synagogue to weep over the destruction of the Temple. I even asked my father to find me a teacher who could guide me in the study of the Cabala; and he selected a man from among the poor." *La Nuit* ought to be read in its entirety, for Elie Wiesel can help us to understand, humanly speaking, what the Child Jesus could have been like.

With Christ, however, authority is always the striking characteristic; even as a child, He already speaks as one having authority. He questions the doctors; but He dazzles them with His own answers. The light that came into this world is here manifested, just as it was manifested in the manger: it rose for a few hours out of the shadows which soon, however, encircled it again.

It is possible to catch an inkling of how the boy Jesus was totally given to His Father in the walls of his home at Nazareth. Everything is summed up in one sentence from Saint Luke: "And Jesus advanced in wisdom and age and grace before God and men." And the Virgin "kept all these things carefully in her heart." Luke tells us nothing further. But legend, strikingly, did not take advantage of his silence; it did not fill the void. Luke himself had learned nothing notable about these thirty years. He therefore recorded nothing—he who told us everything about the mystery of Christmas. His silence concerning the hidden life of Nazareth authenticates the Gospel of the Annunciation and of the Holy Night, and all those things which he could have learned only from Mary. On this matter we must remember the scrupulosity which Luke manifested at the beginning of his narrative: "Inasmuch as many have undertaken to draw up a narrative concerning the things that have been fulfilled among us, even as they who from the beginning were eyewitnesses and ministers of the word have handed them down to us, I also have determined, after following up all things carefully from the very first, to write for thee. . . ."

Thirty years of entombment in a closely knit

Jewish family in an obscure town, plus only three brief years to spread fire upon the earth: "I have come to cast fire upon the earth and what will I but that it be kindled?" What patience before such impatience! What slowness before such haste! What immobility before that hurried race which extends from the baptism of John to the agony, to the scourging, to spittle, and to ignominious death!

At certain moments, perhaps, Mary asked herself if she had not merely dreamed what she pondered in her heart. All the while Christ remained a boy with a heart like ours and a body destined to suffering. He completely understood this suffering ahead of time: He who was a man, the man whose divinity hides His manhood from us today. He remained a Jewish artisan like other men, although He was undoubtedly more pious than the others (even among the Essenes and Pharisees there were many holy people): He for whom time did not exist, whose whole divinity was plunged into an eternal present, He had to live thirty years awaiting a fate which He knew in every detail. He knew that He would be rejected and that He would find only a handful of people to help Him change the world.

Our faith stumbles before the scandal of this failure. We know, however, that love does not force itself upon us: the love of the Son of Man no more than any other. Love demands hearts which either hold back or give themselves. God is love; it is for this reason that He can be rejected. If He forced Himself upon creatures He would not be God; and man would not be the proud individual alone in creation who can turn his head from left to right in a sign of refusal. All Christian life is contained in this consent, once given and never withdrawn; love does not take by force the being it loves. It invites; it solicits; and this is primarily the role of grace.

Grace, however, does more than invite or solicit; and in this respect it differs from human love: it acts within us. There is no man, if he knew how to express himself and if he knew himself, who could not trace the parabola of this pursuit in his life and who could not point to a given moment in his past where he was called by name. Someone was there; He has always

38

been there; but we preferred everything—even anything—to Him. It is only in the desert that comes at the end of life, in the aridity of old age, that even those who were more or less faithful and who followed the Lord from afar can really choose Him: there is no one else, there is nothing else left.

*Dominus meus et Deus meus! My Lord and my God!* I do not utter this cry to You as Thomas did after Your Resurrection or with the intention of putting my fingers into Your wounds; I adore You even before You do a single thing, even while You were still living in that obscure kitchen of Nazareth where You waited—in that dark stall which was like the enclosure where the bull hears the tumult of a bloodthirsty crowd before charging into the blinding sunlight of the arena.

It was in such obscurity that Charles de Foucauld understood the mystery of his vocation. Christ lived at Nazareth; and for any victim what precedes martyrdom is more difficult to suffer than martyrdom itself. The expectation of the chalice is agony; Jesus at Nazareth was already in His agony. The knowledge of failure before having undertaken anything, of refusal before having asked anything, of accepting the mystery of evil which will not be vanquished because it can be preferred (otherwise God would not be love): the whole hidden life of the Lord was perhaps passed in such knowledge and in such consent. And if He was called Jesus of Nazareth during His public life, *Nazareth* resounds in this name not as a reminder of the place where He lived, but as the title of a signal nobility: the nobility of an artisan stretched out and crucified in spirit beforehand, perhaps even upon the pieces of wood that His poor worker's hands had hewn.

What Charles de Foucauld was looking for at Nazareth was, according to Father Huvelin, the one last place that no one has ever been able to steal from Christ. But I wonder if Father de Foucauld's view of such "abjection"—the word recurs often under his pen—corresponds to the reality of Christ's life. There was something worse than "abjection" (as Charles de Foucauld understands it) for the Son of Man in Nazareth: He lived a normal life among a society of people, in a large family, and within a group who would later look upon Him as a fool and seek means to apprehend Him! "But when his own people had heard of it, they went out to lay hold of him." (Mark 3:21) "For not even his brethren believed in him." (John 7:5)

When Charles de Foucauld expressed his famous resolution—"For me, to seek always the last of the last places, to arrange my life in such a way as to be the last, the most despised of men"—his vow, however heroic, belied a desire to be in the first place, since the first shall be the last. But Jesus of Nazareth occupied the place that belonged to Him: it was neither high nor low; but it was His and not another's. ("And they said: Is this not Jesus, the son of Joseph, whose father and mother we know?") He was like all others, distinguishing Himself from them neither by voluntary abjection nor even perhaps by His way of life. He was probably invited to many weddings before that of Cana; perhaps He figured frequently among the friends of the bride. Yet He was the Christ, the Son of the Living God. Only in the desert, nourished on locusts, would He ever feel delivered of His human nature and thus given to the Father. Life within the confines of a Jewish family, one that was poor but respected, was His unimaginable trial—one which many young people can readily understand. Such, for instance, was Rimbaud who was "the only witness of his glory and his reason."

Christ loved these people, however, and He loved each one of them individually, in a very intense manner, just as later He loved the sons of Zebedee. He had taken on flesh but not sinful flesh, although this distinction does not mean that His love was limited in any way. The Son of God took upon Himself everything in man that is capable of involvement and suffering.

At Nazareth Christ is our brother insofar as we belong to a certain family, to a milieu, to a particular profession, to a city, and to a class from which we cannot in good conscience dissociate ourselves. For this reason the Son of Man was first suspect to many around Him and then very quickly hated. He was the Son of Mary; His friends were well known; yet He claimed to be a prophet! These were the beginnings of that accusation which would lead to his crucifixion: "that being a man, He made Himself like to God."

Christ manifested Himself to the world so that He could be known to the greatest number of people. But He was never so alone as when He was in a crowd, unless perhaps it was when He was with the Twelve who hoped for His earthly triumph and even disputed among themselves for the first place in His kingdom. They did not understand that the kingdom was not of this world, that it is within us. They will understand this only when the Spirit transforms them at Pentecost. But while the Son of Man lives He will remain unrecognized, even unknown.

I sometimes have the impression that Christ found in creatures only what He Himself had put there. His visible miracles are the sign of this greater invisible miracle that is constantly renewed: the sign of a poor soul touched and won over by a mere look. The proof of this is found in the words: "Thy sins are forgiven," sovereignly pronounced (the visible miracle comes after these words and is intended to establish the reality of the absolution in which God is revealed). If it takes God Himself to forgive the sins of man, then man realizes what they are and is horrified by them; he repents and he loves; his soul is healed before his body. In reading the Gospels I sometimes have the feeling that, with the exception of His Mother, the Son of Man was really understood only by the man born blind or by the good thief on the cross. These people saw Him and knew Him because He gave them the power to do so. I am not, of course, forgetting Saint Peter's confession: "Thou art the Christ . . ." But before Pentecost were not human considerations much more bound up with the faith of the Apostles?

*O my God, never less alone than when You withdraw from the crowd and from the disciples too, You found it necessary to isolate Yourself in order to pray! And we who love You, miserable as we are, experience the solitude that was Yours in the midst of men and that rewarding presence which fills us as soon as we are alone.*

*You say quickly what You have to say. You "spread fire upon the earth." You do quickly what You have to do (according to the counsel which You gave Judas on the last evening of Your life),*

44

*anxious to reach that day and that hour when the sign of the Son of Man will be authenticated forever. We, too, are impatient to enter with You into the shadows of Your last night.*

# III

# The Mystery of the Cross

THE event which Christians commemorate during the week called Holy belongs to history and not to myth. Those for whom the religious is always mythical tend to forget this important fact. Reported to us by numerous texts which generations of exegetes have studied, the event takes place under Tiberius in an age not too distant from our own—for what, after all, is two thousand years?—and in that section of the East which we define today as "Near."

This event concerns a man altogether like us, but a Semite: one born of a people with whom we still deal today, though we Christians very often forget this fact because we adore Christ as God. But we must also believe that the Son of God was the Son of Man: a man, and not just any man, but an artisan with the nature and the character of a man.

He lived His obscure youth as a worker in a village. Around His thirtieth year He abruptly emerged from this shadow and traveled through Galilee first and then Judea as a healer and a teacher. There had been others who did this before Him; there are still some who do it to-day. But what Christ accomplished immediately caused even the poor to believe what He told them. And what was it that He told them? "Heaven and earth will pass away, but my words will not pass away." And indeed they have not passed away; they still fire us; they have created a new humanity; for generations of believers they have changed hearts of stone into hearts of flesh. And for many, even after they have lost the faith, the hearts of flesh remain.

When I wrote my *Life of Jesus*, Christ's outstanding characteristics impressed me more and more as I advanced in my work. How, I thought, could anyone maintain the idea that Jesus was "a mythical person"? At times I thought that I could hear His voice gently reproving those

around Him. He seemed to shrug His shoulders
and to sigh heavily when those closest to Him
persisted in understanding nothing of what He
had come to do here below. He was, of course,
violent too but His violence was that of love.
"I have come to cast fire upon the earth and
what will I but that it be kindled?" Once ignited
this fire never went out; it continues today to
frighten the masters of the world. Though the
word "revolutionary" is abused and tainted and
we are reluctant to apply it to Christ, He was
nevertheless the first of an immense posterity:
One who loved His human brothers more than
His own life.

The Passion of Christ concerns all mankind
because it tells us that a human being presumed
to take upon himself, in the period of one night
and one day, the suffering of all men. We have
not all been betrayed by a kiss; we have not all
been renounced by our best friend and abandoned by others; we have not all been nailed
to a cross; we have not all had the spittle of
policemen and soldiers hurled in our faces or
suffered the weight of the enormous fists; we

48

have not all been humiliated and scorned because of our nationality. We have not all failed, as the Crucified failed, on this evening of the Sabbath, even to the point where that cry which shakes our faith was torn from Him, torn from a body which was nothing but one gaping wound: "My God, my God, why hast thou forsaken me?"

It was not enough that He suffer this total martyrdom: it was He who called it down upon Himself. Throughout the three Synoptics, as throughout the fourth Gospel, in words which could not have been invented (we can hear His voice tremble), He makes it clear that He knows exactly what awaits Him; He foretells the chalice which He will drink.

The poor who followed Him, and who had built their hopes on Him, would have taken flight had He suddenly revealed to them what He must suffer, and they with Him, before entering His kingdom. For it was indeed a question of conquering a kingdom, of a promised victory over the world. This is what deceived the naive fishermen who abandoned their nets and boats: "Fear not, I have overcome the world." But this victory was closely linked to a defeat: it was in fact an immense victory arising out of a total defeat. This is precisely what we commemorate during Holy Week and it cannot be denied by anyone. Believers or not, we agree upon the reason for this strange contradiction which causes such a triumph to come out of such a disaster. Those who do not believe that a crucified Jew arose from the dead will at least admit that His disciples believed it, that this certitude changed their despair into joy and, suddenly, transformed cowards into bold martyrs.

## *Jesus Is Taken Captive*

What, then, was this Jesus of Nazareth during the last week of His life? The fourth Gospel makes it clearer than the Synoptics: He was an outcast forced into hiding.

The priests had already judged and condemned this blasphemer, this Galilean from the lower classes who, being man, had made Himself like God: He had dared to forgive sins. They had no hesitation or doubt about Him. But He might go further: under some bold illumination, perhaps, He would strive for supreme power. To play the Messiah is to play the conquerer. But the Romans were there and Pilate, their procurator, did not like the Jews.

Pilate ruled with a heavy hand. The time had come to deliver the redoubtable leader to him— He who surely possessed some special power. The priests on their part felt certain that this power came from Beelzebub.

Jesus had remained within Herod's precincts, enjoying some safety, until the death of His friend Lazarus recalled Him to Bethany. But He knew what was being plotted against Him because Nicodemus, another of His friends, was a member of the Council. Jesus was a kind of convict who, though prohibited from entering the Temple, yet was obliged to go there during the feast of the Passover. It was at that moment that He was seized. Perhaps His enemies thought He believed Himself to be safe because the people surrounded and acclaimed Him. Yet His very entrance into the city under the palms and among the hosannas brought about His downfall. The priests had Him seized at the hour of darkness; one of Christ's closest friends was, in fact, on their side, working with them.

Before Christ underwent the suffering of this night (which began in agony instead of ending with it, as though it were necessary that He experience agony by Himself and that it precede the betrayal by His friend), an act took place which forever fixes the mysterious folly of the Christian faith. This was the Last Supper.

The Lord's last meal in this world was really an anticipation of His resurrection. Before being delivered and immolated, He broke bread and said to those who were gathered around Him: "This is my body, which is being given for you." Blood still flowed in His veins when He blessed the chalice which contained a little wine and said: "This cup is the new covenant in my blood, which shall be shed for you."

Is this really a myth? If so, it is one born from the first day of Christianity. What we know about it is founded upon very ancient testimony that is prior to that of the Synoptics. Saint Paul wrote to the Corinthians: "For I myself have received from the Lord (what I also delivered to you), that the Lord Jesus, on the night in which he was betrayed, took bread, and giving thanks broke, and said, 'This is my body which shall be given up for you; do this in remembrance of me.' In like manner also the cup, after he had supped, saying, 'This cup is the new covenant in my blood; do this as often as you drink it, in remembrance of me."

What will become the Sacrifice of the Mass is already, from the dawn of the Church, the living Bread around which the Church will weave, to enfold herself in it, a seamless robe of doctrine, definitions, and rites. The Eucharist was at the center of everything from the very beginning. And on the day after the Resurrection, as the Acts of the Apostles states specifically, the disciples continued "daily with one accord in the temple, and breaking bread in their houses, they took their food with gladness and simplicity of heart."

After His last word over a cup of wine God emptied Himself, and followed by a few frightened men, he passed through Cedron in the night; He became the outcast; He became the convict who will forever be banished from certain places. The little group entered the olive orchard where they were accustomed to spend the night when they did not have enough time to reach Bethany.

Overcome with fatigue, the disciples went to sleep on the ground; Christ began to watch and pray.

What Christian, at some moment in his life, has not reflected in his heart and in his mind upon the reality of this nightly watch: each word, each sign, each drop of sweat and blood? Who has not heard the sound of footsteps and listened to voices in the shadows?

Here is the friend who will betray Him; here is the retinue of the high priest; here are the tribune and the soldiers of the cohort. None of them could have distinguished one of these Jews from another had not the kiss of Judas designated him. They were all alike—*these despicable, dark-skinned rats!* Those who apprehended Christ must have used some such derogatory language to appease a contempt which even in our day Christians are only *beginning* to be ashamed of.

Judas consummates the betrayal with a kiss. The others take flight. The Lamb of God is delivered into hands which we surely know: hands which have never ceased to busy themselves in reformatories, in concentration camps, and in police courts. Yet there is not one affront, not one gob of spittle on this adorable Face that matches the horror of Peter's triple denial when he, squatting near the fire (for this spring night was chilly) in the courtyard of the high priest, is questioned by a servant and replies: "I do not know this man; I do not know who he is."

It was the hatred of the priests which delivered Jesus to the legalistic scrupulosity of the civil servant. A Jew, Pilate thought, is only a Jew; but the Romans have principles and, anyway, this Jew is different from the others. Pilate wanted to release Christ; he was, however, a man of politics; he had a career to look out for. We know Pilate's type: Pilate is one of those who are always in line for a promotion. He must deal with many people, even with this rabble from the temple, because they can cause harm. Herod, too, is dangerous. The people are thrown into confusion and a report from Herod delivered in high places could have major consequences. "And after all, am I a Jew? Let them handle this thing themselves. I wash my hands of it." And Pilate continues to wash his hands—even after two thousand years.

We can understand what this "washing of

hands" means if we reflect on the endless chain of injustices and human ferocity that defines history, and if we observe all the honest people who have chosen, on their part, to overlook these things. *And what do we do?*

### Brother of All the Condemned

What purpose would it serve to trace the way of the Cross here? It is well known to everyone. Even atheists, with a sidelong glance, follow this being, this brother of all the condemned who still suffer. I have always liked the words which the barbarian Clovis shouted to Remi (who had related the story of the Crucifixion to him): "If I had only been there with my Franks!" If we had only been there! But we are there, if it is true that Christ will be in agony until the end of the world and if He is present, as He said He would be, in all those who suffer.

Let us pass on immediately to the final defeat, the last demonstration of absolute impotence on the part of the Hebrew imposter who pretended to raise up the dead, to read minds, and to forgive sins. The doctors and the scribes are about to shout at Him to come down from the Cross: then they will believe! He cured others but He cannot cure Himself! What mockery! They almost choked themselves in laughter! His mother is there, together with some women and John (who testifies to this); and suddenly they hear that great and mysterious cry—a cry which is enough to make the centurion strike his breast and believe that this criminal is the Messiah come into the world.

## To the Inn at Emmaus

All has been said and the story is finished; yet the story is also about to begin. A man may not believe that Christ rose from the dead, but he cannot deny that Christ's friends believed it. They believed they saw Him, that they lived with Him after His death: all this is indisputable.

Let us set aside for a moment the testimonies of the Synoptics and the fourth Gospel, for these books permit various readings and a certain vagueness is perceptible in them. We shall go straight to an anterior testimony, to the first one of all. It was Saint Paul who recalled these words to the Corinthians: "For I delivered to you first of all, what I also received, that Christ died for our sins according to the Scriptures, and that he was buried, and that he rose again the third day, according to the Scriptures, and that he appeared to Cephas, and after that to the Eleven. Then he was seen by more than five hundred brethren at one time, many of whom are with us still, but some have fallen asleep. After that he was seen by James, then by all the apostles. And last of all, as by one born out of due time, he was seen also by me."

It is true that Saint Paul fails to mention the testimony of those women who figure prominently in the Gospels. Again he speaks of the apparition to James which is mentioned only in the apocryphal writings. But it is by beginning with this evidence of Saint Paul that we must analyze in detail and meditate upon the Gospels of the Resurrection.

It seems to me there is one page of the Gospel for each one of us. Some weep with Mary Magdalene before the empty tomb and suddenly He appears: a man who pronounces their names in a low voice. Others put their fingers in the open wounds with Thomas. For my part, I have walked all my life with the two tired travelers who entered Emmaus in the evening. Christ was dead; they had lost everything. Only now, when the shadows of my life are deepening, do I understand what I wrote twenty years ago on this subject in my *Life of Jesus:* "Who among us is not familiar with the inn at Emmaus? Who has not walked on this road in the evening when all seemed lost? Christ was dead within us. They had taken Him from us—the world, the philosophers and sages, our passions. There was no Jesus for us on the earth. We followed a road, and Someone walked at our side. We were alone and yet we were not alone. It was evening. Here was an open door, the obscurity of a room where the flame from the fireplace lighted nothing but the trampled earth and made the shadows flicker. O broken bread! O breaking of the bread, consummated in spite of so much misery! 'Stay with us . . . the day declineth . . .' The day declineth, life is coming to a close. Childhood seems further away than the beginning of the world; and our lost youth means no more to us than the last sound in the dead trees of an unknown park. . . ."

## You Did It to Me

Christians believe that the risen Christ did not leave the world. Paul saw Him, in the literal sense of the word. And in other ways Christ has shown Himself in the course of the centuries to many saints, to the simple faithful, and even to the unbaptized, like Simone Weil. But the greatest number have not seen and have believed: we believe that Christ is actually living. This is indeed the "Christian folly."

What evidence do those who believe that Christ is living and who nevertheless have not seen Him have for affirming the absurd? Whence comes this conviction? How does this presence manifest itself in a life? In the beginning, certainly, there is an act of faith in a revealed word confirmed by interior experience. "Peace I leave with you, my peace I give to you; not as the world gives do I give to you." This living peace is not a trap: the Christian knows it and lives it. It is linked to the state of grace which, as long as we remain in it, verifies the fulfillment of the promise: "If anyone love me, he will keep my word, and my Father will love him, and we will come to him and make our abode with him." Above all, the Christian can, if he is a Catholic, avail himself each day of that morsel of bread about which the Lord pronounced words so foolish ("I am the living bread . . .") that the disciples mumured and, Saint John tells us, many of those who heard them no longer wanted to follow Him. Yet for over two thousand years generations of faithful have lived on this bread that was broken and multiplied for them.

The living Christ also gives Himself to those who do not believe or who scoff at this folly and hate it, provided they are worthy of Him. For Christ identified Himself with the hungry man to whom we give something to eat or whom we refuse. "I am this hungry man; I am this stranger; I am this man in prison whom you visited or tortured."

Each one of us ought to reread chapter twenty-five of the Gospel according to Matthew. "As long as you did it for one of these my least brethren, you did it for me." This is the sacrament of those who serve Christ without knowing Him and who love Him in their brothers. We must always come back to the words of Saint John of the Cross: "In the evening of life, we will be judged on love." Indeed, Love Itself will be our Judge.

### The Holy Face

Each one of us has his own idea of Jesus as a man, apart from the matter of belief in His Divinity. This conception of Him is highly personal, even incommunicable. The Church leaves her children free: they may transfigure "the most beautiful of the sons of men" into a glorious Messiah or adore the Nazarene who passed for a fool among His own people; they may contemplate the crucified victim whose unrecognizable face was already prophesied by Isaias. We represent to ourselves the Jesus whom our nature solicits and whom our love demands. We re-create Him, certainly not in our image and likeness, but according to the need we have of being inspired in His presence.

Christ, however, really lived on earth and belongs to history. We must, therefore, recognize

that either one of two ideas is true: if those who
believe in a Christ of noble and majestic appearance are right, then those who imagine Him
to be weak and without grandeur are wrong.
Both aspects of the Incarnate Christ find some
justification in the Gospels. But one fact seems
to dominate the whole question: Jesus was not
recognized by the majority of people. He as-
serted Himself so infrequently that His enemies
hesitated to oppose Him. He seems to have influenced the crowds much more by His words
and by His miracles than by His appearance or
attitudes. From the beginning of His public life
those who did not believe in His preaching or in
His miracles discerned nothing of the divine in
the traits of His countenance. The Samaritan
woman at first saw only an ordinary Jew in the
stranger and she made fun of Him. His enemies,
in no way intimidated and already murderers,
were sparing with Him only because they feared
the people; but there was no doubt in their minds
that they were dealing with an impostor. When
Judas delivered Him to them, he did not say:
"You will recognize Him by His stature. The
one who stands a head over all others and whose

majesty is obvious to the eye is the one who is to be seized." He did not say: "You will at once notice the Leader and the Master." It was necessary that a kiss single Him out, for even with their torches, the soldiers could not distinguish Him among the eleven poor Jews who were around Him.

It is nevertheless true that Christ was many times loved at first sight and that He was often followed by people as soon as He began to speak, even before He performed any miracle. One call was enough to make some men abandon all they possessed in this world and follow Him. He sometimes arrested people's attention with an irresistible eye; His omnipotence was affirmed each time that a repentant creature fell to His knees in the dust.

In this apparent opposition between a Christ who, merely by drawing near, captured hearts and a Nazarene agitator despised by the rulers and priests and who could not be distinguished from His disciples by the soldiers charged with His arrest, in this contradictory vision we must try to discover what the human appearance of Christ really was.

Undoubtedly He was like many people whose beauty, at once very secret and very striking, dazzled some and escaped others; this is especially true when beauty is of the spiritual order. The august light on this face could be perceived only by an interior disposition. When we are in love, we are often surprised by the indifference others show to the face which, for us, sums up all the splendor of the world. Many do not even think of looking at those characteristics of Christ which reflected heaven, the mere sight of which makes us wild with delight and anguish. The least moment spent with the loved one is of inestimable value to us; yet it often makes little difference to his companions or his parents to live under the same roof with him or to share in the same work and breathe the air which he breathes.

Like all creatures, Christ is transformed by the person who is attracted to Him. To this very natural phenomenon grace adds its unpredictable action. We cannot appear to another person as we would like him to see us, but the God-Man is not only the master of hearts but also the master of grace that is at work in hearts. He cured many more men born blind than the Gospel recounts. Each time a creature called Him his Lord and his God and confessed that He was the Christ, the Messiah come into this world, he did so because Christ had opened the interior eye whose vision is not limited simply to appearances.

For this reason, Rembrandt, of all the painters, seems to me to have given Christ an image most in conformity with the evangelical account. I am thinking especially of the oil painting in the Louvre where a tired and almost anemic God is recognized by the two disciples with whom He breaks bread in the inn at Emmaus. Nothing could be more ordinary than that suffering face. One might dare say that there is nothing more common. Yet this humble countenance is resplendent with a light whose source is the Father: Love itself. No one could be more a man than this poor Nazarene whom the priests mocked so terribly and who, even before the scourging disfigured Him, appeared so unimposing before the bodyguards and hirelings that even one of the high priest's servants gave Him a blow. Yet in this miserable flesh looming out of an abyss of humiliation and torture, God shines forth with mild and terrible grandeur. Everything seems to happen as though the miracle of the Transfiguration was not accomplished once on Thabor but was renewed as many times as it pleased the Lord to make Himself known to one of His creatures.

Whether a man is loved or not, adored or despised, he possesses a certain figure which cannot be altered a single cubit. He appears erect or humped; his features are regular or deformed. His hair and his eyes have a certain color. It would seem that we have a document which, if authentic, would end all discussion concerning the physical appearance of the Lord, since it would furnish us with a literal photograph of it. I am not competent to discuss the problem raised by the Holy Shroud of Turin and by the image of the crucified man imprinted upon it. I have pictures of it; I have heard and read the impressive commentaries of Paul Vignon, who was both scholar and apostle. If we accept as true this image whose manifestation was reserved to the present century (due to one of those discoveries our age is so proud of), we can no

67

longer deny that Christ was of majestic stature and that His august countenance invoked adoration, perhaps, more than love.

What is strange is that, by a mysterious filiation, almost all the images of the triumphant Christ which painters have invented from the first Byzantine effigies to the Christs of Giotto and Angelico, of Raphael and Titian, or of Quentin Metsys resemble the mysterious design contained in the Holy Shroud whose existence was not even suspected by any of the innumerable artists who painted Christ. Indeed it has the countenance on which everyone is agreed and which comes to mind when we say of someone: "He has a head like Christ." Even today the most insipid imagery of the area of Saint-Sulpice dishonors the authentic face as it appeared to the Virgin, to Magdalene, and to John; this makes the crime of that place so much greater. Saint-Sulpice has caricatures of Christ rather than portraits of Him; well do we turn our eyes away when we pass by its showcases. If, however, the relic of Turin is authentic, the Son of Man probably resembles the rose statues of Sacré-Coeur.

On the other hand, the early painters who

were fond of depicting the suffering and hu-miliated Christ as He was before His passion—and even as He remained throughout the horrors of the scourging, the crowning with the thorns, the crucifixion, and the agony—have exaggerated their case. They have blurred the real physical beauty of Christ. On the Shroud of Turin, stained with pus and blood, that beauty still shines forth. The most atrocious death has left Christ's body intact; and the blows, the spittle, the blood, and the tears did not destroy the purity of His in-corruptible face for even a single moment.

# IV

# The Presence of the Risen Christ

A MAN was born in Judea in the time of Augustus; he died and was buried in Jerusalem under the reign of Tiberius; yet the death of this man did not interrupt His life. Anyone rash enough to undertake an account of His life does not know where to stop; for the tomb where this criminal's body was placed is not really the end of anything. His sepulcher is but a marker beside a road which, in the course of human history, becomes progressively broader.

Even those who deny the historical reality of Christ's resurrection will admit that during the few weeks following His death His disciples believed that they saw Him, that they spoke with Him, that they encountered Him in definite places: on a village road in the evening or in a garden on the edge of a lake where they were fishing. *While they were at table behind closed doors, Christ entered and one of them put his fingers in the wounds of His hands, His feet, and His heart.* Whether or not they were under an illusion, they were convinced that they had seen Him; and their certitude transformed the cross of the crucified, which was a scandal and an opprobrium, into a source of hope so abundant that even today it slakes our thirst. "For I delivered to you first of all," Saint Paul wrote in his first letter to the Corinthians in which he spoke of events known to all and which required no elaboration, "what I also received, that Christ died for our sins according to the Scriptures, and that he was buried, and that he rose again the third day, according to the Scriptures, and that he appeared to Cephas, and after that to the Eleven. Then he was seen by more than five hundred brethren at one time, many of whom are with us still, but some have fallen asleep. After that he was seen by James, then by all the apostles. And last of all, as by one born out of due time, he was seen also by me."

The second and very short life of Christ, which

extends from the Resurrection to the Ascension, confirmed the faith of the apostles and gave the thirty hidden as well as the three public years of the Jewish preacher's life infinite significance: His tomb had become a cradle. One evening in an inn at Emmaus becomes a ray of dawn which breaks over the first chalice.

But we do not know where to end this second life any more than the first, for it, too, has no fixed term. It is followed by a third life which began when the risen Christ had scarcely disappeared into the clouds, a life that continues today: the invisible Master's occupation of all roads leading into the hearts and souls of men. Here again, whether this presence be real or illusory, it is believed as a fact; it is something that is evident to millions of human beings. To-day, after so many centuries, this man is still there—chosen, betrayed, abandoned, rediscovered, like a friend or like a lover. He remains just as we know Him in the Gospels, with His inordinate demands, separating man from woman and woman from man, destroying the human couple to the scandal of many. All the words He spoke during His mortal life are audible to us. The fire He came to kindle upon the earth has become a conflagration which sometimes flares up before our eyes but which most often smolders and creeps, something like those underground fires in the heath that spread through the roots and turf. It would be an astonishing mystery if people, being so deeply moved, are merely victims of a mirage: such people, for example, as the sisters dedicated to human misery in hospitals, asylums, and leprosariums.

But this work can be explained: a natural vocation, it can be said, inclines the weakest among us toward human suffering. But what about those who separate themselves from the living to belong solely to a man named Jesus who left this world nearly two thousand years ago? For them Christ is always there, more present to them than any visible creature: they are literally nourished by Him. Extreme cases, it may be argued, morbid cases. Yet, even apart from the consecrated, there are a small number of people in all classes, even in the least Christian of all, the working class, and among boys at the age of puberty who sacrifice all other love for the love of a man whom they do not see but who is there, tyrannically present for each one of them.

If you still consider this to be folly, these people will not blame you; for "the folly of the cross," ever since Saint Paul's time, is a meaningful expression among Christians. It could be called an unnatural folly were it not that the protest of man's total being against his apparent nature reveals another need in him, a need of his deepest nature which was already manifest before Christ came with His yoke and with His cross.

### Paul's Testimony

About the year 59, Portius Festus, governor of Judea, found a man named Paul in the prison of Caesarea; his predecessor Felix had held him there for two years. Festus, explaining Paul's situation to King Agrippa, who was a Jew, summarized it in this way: "There is a certain man left a prisoner by Felix, and when I was at Jerusalem, the chief priests and elders of the Jews presented their case against him and asked for his conviction. But I told them that Romans are not accustomed to give any man up before

the accused has met his accusers face to face
and has been given a chance to defend himself
against the charges. Therefore, when they had
assembled here, I lost no time, but on the following day took my seat on the tribunal and
ordered the man to be brought in. But when his
accusers got up, they did not charge him with
any of the crimes that I had expected. But they
had against him certain questions about their
own religion and *about a certain Jesus, who had
died, but who Paul affirmed was alive.*"

Just as on Easter evening Christ was dead and
yet living, so on Ascension evening He returned
to His Father but He did not leave His own.
The signs of His presence are found everywhere.
By "signs" I do not mean those striking testimonies of Christian genius that stand out as land-
marks in universal history, but rather a presence,
something like an underground stream, which
comes to the surface at certain moments. Human
ears hear a voice or believe that they hear it;
men and women speak of something that has
been said: and sometimes we recognize this, or
believe that we recognize it. The man whose
name is Jesus and around whom the Gospels

75

center is not a disincarnate creature; He possesses a definite, clean-cut character and He said
nothing that did not have a particular tonality—
so much so that the "words of the Lord" (which
were first transmitted orally) retain a kind of
tremor in which their tone and accent remain
perceptible. If, then, Paul was not deceived in
affirming to Festus that the Crucified still lived,
we ought to be able to recognize that tone and
that accent in what a Gertrude, a Theresa, or an
Angela of Foligno tell us about their conversations with the Lord. My own quest, my own
confrontation with the Christ of the Gospel, with
the invisible and omnipresent Christ who puts
His trust in His loved ones, was inspired by
a passion which, though it may not have been
totally pure, took its strength from the weakness
of my faith. I desired to prove to myself that the
Jesus of Emmaus is always there, in the heart
of this dark world, and that He dwells with us
in this stifling twilight. Since other men and
women hear Him and repeat what they have
heard, I flattered myself that I, too, recognized
His voice; after all, I had been familiar with

that voice since childhood and belong to His fold.

But the words of the invisible Lord reported by the saints do not have the nudity of those which, in the days of Herod and Tiberius, re-sounded in Judea. Even when the words of these people have not gone through abysses of medi-ocrity and inanity before reaching us, they are often translated and interpreted by creatures whose natural gifts do not equal their virtue. Above all, they are confused with many others that are the fruit of pious imagination; a totally divine water wells up in the midst of humanity: water at once pure and muddy, mingled with debris and leaves. This becomes apparent as soon as we read *Les Divines Paroles*, a book in which Father Saudreau endeavors to clarify what Christ really said to those close to Him in the course of Christian centuries.

In this light we can understand the discretion of Saint Theresa in Chapter Three of her *Sixth Mansion* where she treats "of the words which God addresses to the soul and the marks by which they can be distinguished from those which come from the imagination or the devil." Of all these marks, simplicity and clarity are what especially strike us as characteristic of each authentic precept of Christ. In spite of the devotional nature of much language, however, we can occasionally break through to its clear and simple meaning. Saint Theresa does not speak of this nudity of the divine words as the sign that helps us to recognize them, but she must have been aware of the difficulty. She writes: "A soul finds itself in pain, in trouble, and these few words: *do not be troubled*, calm it, fill it with light and dissipate all its troubles—troubles from which, a few moments before, it would not have believed the wisest men in the world could have delivered it. Another person is in affliction and in fear; he hears only these words: *It is I, fear not*, and suddenly all of his apprehensions disappear. Another is worried about the success of some important business, and hears these words: *peace be to you. . . .*"

*Be not troubled, it is I, fear not, peace be to you*—this is the human language God uses when He speaks to suffering man, as to the sea troubled in its depths. Immediately there is a great calm; in this calm the Master is recognized. This is human language at the extremity of simplicity and efficacy, reduced almost to nothing: language which is on the edge of a living silence and which Christ always uses to talk to His creatures. Brief flashes with deep interior meaning open new perspectives to those whom Christ loves: perspectives of silence, of night, of nothingness. Like the Samaritan woman, other women linger by similar wells to speak with Incarnate Truth; but Saint John of the Cross distrusts even these delights—not that he rejects or disdains interior words which he calls "substantial" and which, he says, invade the soul to the point of becoming its whole strength and its whole life. But Saint John remains the lover of love in the night: love according to him is the fruit of faith, that is to say, of darkness. He distrusts whatever removes a soul from "obscure faith where the understanding must be left behind in order to go to God by love." Thus, to follow in the footsteps of the invisible Christ in His third life, it is not sufficient to overhear the dialogues of the Son with His creature; we must also interpret each silence.

## The Mystical Body

The men and women who barricaded themselves in the upper room when Christ was taken
from them, but who were still close to Him,
even to the point of hearing the vibration of
His last words, were filled with Him and became one with Him. The "mystical body," the
identification of the Church and Christ, was a
very tangible truth during those first weeks. The
Spirit who came over the Apostles caused the
Trinity to dwell in them more completely. "If
anyone love me," Christ had told them, "he will
keep my word, and my Father will love him,
and we will come to him and make our abode
with him." But now Love, too, abides in them.

As soon as they received the Spirit, they manifested God so strikingly that Annas the high
priest, Caiphas, and all the murderers of Christ
who were still there must have believed that
Christ had returned. When the tomb had been
closed over His dead body, there was no doubt
in their minds the affair was finished, not
only because the poor wretch was dead but

especially because the ordeal of His passion had shown Him to be impotent, and therefore both a liar and an imposter. But now, once again, His presence was felt throughout the city. His name spread from mouth to mouth; a lame man had just been cured at the gate of the Temple which was called Beautiful; and on Solomon's porch where yesterday the agitator had dared cry out to the Jews who pressed in on Him: "I and the Father are one"—on that very porch the same crowd was greatly excited by a miracle and surrounded Peter and John. Only a small number believed in the visible Christ; but now that the Apostles spoke in His name, all who heard them were "cut to the heart" as the author of the Acts tells us.

These thousands of baptized men were purchased by Christ's blood; they immediately became diligent in hearing the word, in taking part in the breaking of bread and in prayers. For them the consecrated Host was less a presence than a food. There is no doubt, as Saint Paul's texts prove, that they already believed what we believe today about the Bread of Life and the Chalice of the Lord; but the sense of

Christ's presence was given to them in a special way by the spirit of love: the power over matter and that power over flesh and over hearts which they received from the Lord identified with them.

An unbelievable revulsion suddenly disconcerted the high priests, those foxes caught in their own trap. The infamy of the Cross which crowned the life of Christ now clarifies it, becomes the key to His destiny, the secret to the riddle which He had thrown in their faces during His mortal life. Christ is, said Saint Peter, "the stone that was rejected by you, the builders, which has become the corner stone. Neither is there salvation in any other. For there is no other name under heaven given to men by which we must be saved."

The priests and doctors who had spun the web in which the Son of Man let Himself be taken now began their secret meetings all over again; but this time it was on account of someone who was no longer there. The situation was worse than if He had been there, for He had triumphed over His very execution. Peter and John were arrested and then released; for what could be done against a group which had but one heart and one soul, among whom none owned anything since all things were held in common?

These first brothers of an innumerable family were masters of Solomon's porch even while it was still echoing the words of the Lord. Once again (as in the days of Christ) stretchers were carried out of homes; bodies rested on mats and beds were set up under the sun. The Sanhedrin could well ask themselves what had changed: the Son of Man said a word or used unction or a little mud and spittle to cure the sick; but now it was enough that Peter's shadow pass over them. The invisible Christ no longer seeks to veil His Divinity. He who did not wish to raise legions of angels against His executioners now sends an angel to open the door of the prison where the high priest had once imprisoned Peter and John. Then, for a second time, they preached Christ's resurrection, a doctrine whose very name alone offended all Sadducean ears in the Sanhedrin. This time all the disciples had to appear before the court. The high priest did not dare pronounce the name of his victim before them. "We strictly charged you not to teach in this name," he said.

And he added these words, altogether indicative of the anguish which was beginning to overcome him: "You want to bring this man's blood upon us." The accused, however, remained unperturbed; they began to unravel before him the enigma of Christ's life and death and to demonstrate to this fox that he and all the others had been duped. From that time on, no matter what they did, the high priests would always be known as those to whom the Just One had been delivered; Christ would be known as "the suffering servant" whom Isaias had seen and described to Jews who were both blind and deaf to the truth. "The God of our fathers raised Jesus, whom you put to death, hanging him on a tree. Him God exalted with his right hand to be Prince and Savior, to grant repentance to Israel and forgiveness of sins. . . ." (Acts 5:30)

Through the intervention of a Pharisee named Gamaliel, a Pharisee who believed in the resurrection of the dead, the Apostles were not peremptorily condemned, taken outside, and stoned to death. Gamaliel explained to the Council that if this work came from men it would destroy itself; but if it came from God they must not run the risk of fighting against it. The priests responsible for Christ's death were aware of the terrible character of this risk; but, in spite of their hatred for Christ, they unanimously followed Gamaliel's advice. Gamaliel was a famous doctor and the grandson of the great Hillel, and at this time he had a young man named Saul among his students.

## Stephen and Saul

Saul, Stephen: these two names are inscribed on the threshold of Christ's third life as though to make clear from the outset that mystery of conversion by which Christ has extended His reign. Almost all the stories invented by littérateurs are a history of human loneliness. Loneliness is the foundation for all drama and especially the drama of love. But to the man who is sensitive to the secret of grace, another world is opened up: one which is indivisible from incursions and exchanges, a universe without solitude and where even sin creates bonds between people. In every life that God has entered there can no longer be chance encounters, even when the protagonists are unaware of it. The bee, rising from a flower with pollen-laden feet, is not aware of what it is going to fecundate. *Etiam peccata*, even sins: like a storm, they saturate the heavy atmosphere where souls breathe, seeking one another, damning one another, or saving one another.

## The Face of an Angel

"And Saul approved of his death. . . ." We can never reflect enough upon this perplexing text. Saul, who tomorrow would be Paul devoured by love, agreed that a child of light should be delivered to the mob. He did worse: he co-operated in this savage lapidation. "And the witnesses laid down their garments at the feet of a young man named Saul." (The witnesses threw the first stones.) Perhaps it was necessary that Saul be there that the martyr's eyes could meet his. He was there only for this exchange of glances, to hear the name of Jesus uttered from this mouth covered with blood. And who was Stephen? One of the first upon whom the Twelve imposed hands and who

seemed to be entirely possessed by Christ. He
was resplendent with grace and fortitude: the
most beautiful of the children of men revealed
Himself finally in this child of light and, through
him, multiplied miracles as in the days of His
mortal life; with the same authority, He silenced
the adversaries of the young deacon who had
argued against all the synagogues "of the Freed-
men, and of the Cyrenians and of the Alexandri-
ans and of those from Cilicia and the province
of Asia." His fate was to be resolved as had
been that of the Lord; and their common enemies had recourse to a ruse which had already
been used against Christ: they called upon false
witnesses. Stephen, they said, had blasphemed
against Moses and God. The same scribes and
people who yesterday had roared out at the
death of Christ, now apprehended His disciple
and brought him before the Sanhedrin. They
had accused Christ of saying that He would
destroy the Temple and rebuild it in three days;
they did not look much further to find a reason
to condemn the young deacon: his crime was to
have taught that Christ, the Nazarene, would
destroy the Temple. Then, suddenly, the author

of the Acts, who was perhaps a witness to this event, fixes it in our minds forever: "Then all who sat in the Sanhedrin, gazing upon him, saw his face as though it were the face of an angel."

Saul, too, was probably in this court. What could this "face of light" mean to such a fanatic? Gamaliel's disciple was aware only of the follies Stephen had preached, ones which were abominable to a Jewish ear: all sacred history turned away from its traditional meaning to glorify a Galilean, who a few months earler had been hung on the cross of slaves! Madness rent his heart and he gnashed his teeth like all those who heard this angel provoke the council: "Stiff-necked and uncircumcised in heart and ear, you always oppose the Holy Spirit; as your fathers did, so you do also," he cried, demonstrating that almost furious vehemence which is the proper mark of Christ in the Gospels each time he came up against the eternal Tartuffe,* "Which of the prophets have not your fathers persecuted? And they killed those who foretold the coming of the Just One, of whom you have now been

* A sanctimonious hypocrite, from the name of the title character in Molière's play, Le Tartuffe.

the betrayers and murderers, you who received the Law as an ordinance of angels and did not keep it." As the circle of Jews closed in about him, Stephen raised his eyes and saw Christ.

It was here, nevertheless, that Saul experienced the first touch of grace. The author of the Acts would not have insisted on his presence and the part he took in Stephen's martyrdom if he had not seen in it a point of contact between Saul and Christ. The executioners probably did not cast their garments far from the place where Stephen had been led. Saul, even if he had turned away his head, could not have helped hearing the martyr's prayer: "Lord Jesus, receive my spirit." He did not stop up his ears and the Name he hated must have penetrated his soul, imprinted itself upon him in spite of himself. Stephen spoke to someone Saul did not see; he seemed to speak to no one, but he spoke as though someone were there: "Lord," he still found strength to cry, "do not lay this sin against them." Did Stephen think of one of them in particular, of the most embittered one of all: of Saul who did not deign to do the work of brutes, but who encouraged them, associated him-

self with them, and would travel far to prepare
other massacres? The Father did much more
than grant to Stephen, the first martyr and the
eldest son of an immense family of the immolated, what he dared to ask for: that their crimes
be not imputed to his executioners; with the first
gush of blood a grace was to be born for the
Gentiles, for each one of us, the men of the
West, who belong to the posterity of Paul.

The words of the hidden Christ are not perceptible to us in this first dialogue with one of
His beloved; only those spoken by Stephen are
known to us. But in Stephen's face, as in that
of an angel, the adorable Face was reflected.
Many centuries later, in a little village of Umbria,
at Foligno, the Lord would say to Saint Angela:
"This is the grace I bring you: I desire that
your face be useful to those who see you."
"Who knows what you see!" a woman exclaimed before Benedict Labre when he was in
ecstasy, for a mere glance from him, too, was
sufficient to convert hearts. If Stephen's angelic
aspect stirred only fury in Saul, perhaps it was
because the latter already had to resist an unknown charm. Nothing comes to us from with-

out which is not already in us; and this is especially true with reference to belief in Christ. He Himself said it to Pascal during the unforgettable night: "You would not seek me if you had not already found me."

It will not be a stranger who will suddenly call this man, a few weeks later, on the road to Damascus; even before Saul asks His name, he will already have known that it is the Lord; he will already have recognized that light and that voice which dwelt within him from the time he saw Stephen's angelic face beneath the blood.

The rage which, immediately after Stephen's burial, drove Paul to track down the faithful in their homes and snatch them away was perhaps a protest against what was already impressed upon him and what obsessed him, a protest against the Name which the martyr had pronounced with such ardor and love. Saul, moreover, succumbed to no vile passion: the zeal of the house of God, of the God of Abraham, Isaac, and Jacob possessed him. A profound piety animated him: the piety of a Jew, the same piety which a short while earlier had impelled Christ

to whip the merchants in the temple and to up-
set their money tables. Nothing is less discon-
certing, really, than what is taking place in him;
for he is already on the side of God. And even
if Jesus had not visibly struck him down with
His love, would we have any right to judge
him? We will be astonished one day to see the
persecutors preceding us into the kingdom. Sometimes very noble souls are prevented by their
very nobility from submitting to Christ. They
do not want to yield to the allurement of consolations since they do not believe in them: in
the name of scrupulosity they will say "no"
until the end. Perhaps, without knowing it, they
have that faith which consists in not buying
favors from an unknown God by attitudes and
formulas which neither their reason nor their
hearts can accept. This obdurateness, which is
undoubtedly almost always mingled with pride,
is sometimes a fact of intellectual honesty, courage, and modesty. Saul, certainly, did not lack
faith. On the contrary, he had too much of it;
but it was founded on the impetuosity of his
youth.

Undoubtedly he was surprised by those Jews

who had been transformed into lambs and who let themselves be dragged by him from their homes, who turned the other cheek, and who, fainthearted in appearance, fled whenever they could into the countryside of Judea and Samaria. But they scattered like sparks and a fire was kindled wherever these so-called cowards went. This fire now surrounded Saul; and his violence proved impotent. The weakness of his enemies triumphed on all sides. In Jerusalem only "colonies" were left and the Sanhedrin dared not touch them. But in Samaria, where the woman to whom Jesus had spoken by Jacob's well, telling her that He was the Messiah, undoubtedly still lived, the persecuted Christians must have found some of those she had persuaded to believe in Jesus of Nazareth. Philip was with this little group; and because Philip was there, it was as though Christ had been there. When Philip went out into the streets, impure spirits were cast out. Even a magician, Simon, who was to become one of the first heretics, was part of this group and believed in the name of the Lord. Finally, Peter and John came to lay hands on those who had been baptized.

## *Saul's Conversion*

Saul was so prejudiced against the Apostles and the others who followed the Nazarene that, humanly speaking, there could be little hope of his conversion. But Christ, for the first time since He left the world, is about to manifest Himself personally, without any intermediary between Him and the creature. In the future He will act in this way in more than one life, with less drama but with as much efficacy. When men are not able to do anything, Christ suddenly appears: the victim of a conquering impatience that suffers no interference, He cuts through the knot of difficulties and contradictions with one stroke; it takes Him but an instant to destroy everything that a human being has done for years to resist grace. The Father would never have converted this madman, whom the Gentiles were awaiting in darkness, had not the Son Himself intervened with a kind of haste, a kind of loving impatience. But He will let Saul have one final fling.

The persecutor, "still breathing threats of

slaughter against the disciples of the Lord," had obtained letters to enter the synagogues of Damascus and an escort to bring back to Jerusalem as prisoners all the Christians in that city. We must follow this drama step by step and verse by verse in the text of the Acts: "And as he went on his journey, it came to pass that he drew near to Damascus, when suddenly a light from heaven shone round about him; and falling to the ground, he heard a voice saying to him, 'Saul, Saul, why dost thou persecute me?' And he said, 'Who art thou, Lord?' And he said, 'I am Jesus, whom thou art persecuting. It is hard for thee to kick against the goad.' And he, trembling and amazed, said, 'Lord, what wilt thou have me do?' And the Lord said to him, 'Arise and go into the city, and it will be told thee what thou must do.' Now the men who journeyed with him stood speechless, hearing indeed the voice, but seeing no one. And Saul arose from the ground, but when his eyes were opened, he could see nothing. And leading him by the hand, they brought him into Damascus. And for three days he could not see, and he neither ate nor drank. Now there was in Damascus a certain disciple named Ananias, and the Lord said to him in a vision, 'Ananias.' And he said, 'Here I am, Lord.' And the Lord said to him, 'Arise and go to the street called Straight and ask at the house of Judas for a man of Tarsus named Saul. For behold, he is praying.' (And he saw a man named Ananias come in and lay his hands upon him that he might recover his sight.) But Ananias answered, 'Lord, I have heard from many about this man, how much evil he has done to thy saints in Jerusalem. And here too he has authority from the high priests to arrest all who invoke thy name.' But the Lord said to him, 'Go, for this name is a chosen vessel to me, to carry my name among nations and kings and the children of Israel. For I will show him how much he must suffer for my name.' "

Everything happened as it had been foretold to Ananias: the scales fell from Saul's eyes and he was immediately baptized. After spending a few days with the disciples in Damascus, he began preaching in the synagogues that Jesus was the Son of God; the Jews were dumfounded. They sought means to kill him and they guarded the gates night and day to prevent him from leaving Damascus. But one night the disciples lowered him over the walls of the city in a basket.

Saul, who was now called Paul, went back to Jerusalem. When the faithful saw him they fled. He did not resemble Stephen; his face was not that of an angel; Christ did not radiate from his body; the very sight of him was a cause of terror. This was his first trial: he who wanted to conquer souls created a desert by merely approaching them. As a result, he suffered and wept, not knowing what plans Christ had for him; life in Jerusalem thus became unbearable and he was obliged to leave the holy city. Elsewhere, he believed, other sheep awaited him; and one day while praying in the temple, he received confirmation of this from Christ Himself. This time there was no light from heaven and He who spoke did not have to give His name to be recognized. "I was in an ecstasy," Paul says. What purpose would it serve to find fault with this ecstasy? He saw and heard Christ in the same temple where He Himself had taught and prayed such a short time before. Within him he heard a voice saying, "Make haste and go quickly out of Jerusalem, for they will not receive thy testimony concerning me." "And I said, 'Lord, they themselves know that I used to imprison and beat in one synagogue after another those who believed in thee; and when the blood of Stephen, thy witness, was shed, I was standing by and approved it, and took charge of the garments of those who killed him,' And he said to me, 'Go, for to the Gentiles far away I will send thee.'"

*To the Gentiles far away* . . . This mission concerns each one of us men of the West individually. There are not many generations separating us from our fathers—the Romans, the Iberians—who received the word from Paul or Paul's disciples. And the struggles which Paul had to sustain against the Judaizing Christians show to what degree, from the beginning, he was the herald of the interior Christ: of Him whose footsteps we are trying to trace in this book. Even when the Christians in Jerusalem could no longer doubt that Saul, the persecutor, had been won to Christ they continued to oppose him, even to the point of setting him at odds with James, the brother of the Lord, and with Peter.

### The Thorn in the Flesh

The battle which the Son of Man waged for three years against the letter that kills and in the name of the Spirit which vivifies now takes on its meaning. Paul, who no longer lived anything but the life of Christ ("It is no longer I, but Christ who lives in me"), would henceforward fight to extend, commensurate with the Roman Empire, the frontiers of the kingdom that is within us. He cleared the way to the interior Christ who had, in the midst of the infant Church, no more dangerous adversaries than those Jews of strict observance who were bent on imposing circumcision upon the baptized pagans. In the fold which he could not prevent them from entering, they even went so far as to force the converts to eat in a separate place; and they did so with the approbation of both James and Peter.

Paul taught these newcomers, whose growing

numbers rapidly reduced the influence of the first
Judaizing church of Jerusalem, that the law, the
observances, and anything else that distracted
them from their personal relationship with the
Lord, was worth very little. He did not conceal
from them the secrets of his own life in Christ,
with whom he was so united that there no longer
existed between the servant and the Master any
place for a dialogue as elementary as that on the
road to Damascus. Paul rejoiced in bearing on
his own body the marks of the crucified Christ.
This suffering Jew had what he called a "thorn
in the flesh." Just what this was we can only
conjecture. Who was the "angel of Satan" who
buffeted him? It was an atrocious humiliation,
perhaps both of the physical and spiritual orders,
since this lover of the cross was weakened by it
and prayed that it might depart from him. "My
grace is sufficient for thee," the voice within
him answered, *"for strength is made perfect in
weakness."* Prodigious words, as authentic as
any in the Gospels which, by this divinization
of weakness, erected a stumbling block before
the world against which Nietzsche, in the footsteps of so many other great men, floundered.

The strength which Paul received from the Lord was to transmute all misery into the redemptive cross. Whatever the thorn he speaks of might have been, we know by his own avowal how closely it made him resemble the suffering Christ. "From the Jews five times I received forty lashes less one. Thrice was I scourged . . ."

Not only will he live the passion of his God, step by step; to this will be added what the first martyr, one of whose executioners he had been, suffered: "Once I was stoned . . ." None of the thousand perils he encountered in his voyages mattered—neither hunger, nor cold, nor betrayals; but the Christ in him espoused the innumerable miseries of his flock: "Who is weak, and I am not weak? Who is made to stumble, and I am not inflamed?"

Paul bore all these crosses with a joy that would be incomprehensible to us if we did not know the reasons which he had for belief in Christ. As if the voice heard on the road to Damascus were not sufficient, the interior Master manifested himself in another way: not within Paul's soul this time; rather He literally drew Paul outside of himself. The apostle spoke of this grace to the faithful of Corinth fourteen years after having received it (about the year 42, at the beginning of his ministry when he left Tarsus with Barnabas to evangelize Antioch): "I know a man in Christ who . . . was caught up to the third heaven," he wrote. "And I know such a man—whether in the body or out of the body, I do not know, God knows—that he was caught up into paradise and heard secret words that man may not repeat."

Paul's steadfastness would be unimaginable, just like that of thousands of other martyrs—among whom there are so many virgins, young people, and slaves—without the evidence they had that their Lord and their God was there, within them, unspeakably present. A historian as realistic as Monseigneur Duchesne will admit nothing other than the invisible presence of Christ as an explanation for the triumph of a rigorous, persecuted, and hated doctrine such as early Christianity was. "In certain respects," he writes, "Jesus was present. He lived in His faithful through the Holy Eucharist. In the marvels of charisms, prophecies, visions, ecstasies, and miraculous cures, they still possessed something like a second contact with the invisible divinity. From all this there resulted in the Christian groups and individuals a religious tension, an enthusiasm whose influence must be counted among the most powerful means of conversion. . . ."

To what Monseigneur Duchesne has said, I should like to add another reason for the steadfastness of the early Christians. It was their preoccupation with the imminent return of Jesus: their universal expectation that the Son of Man was at the gates, that He would steal up on them like a thief for final judgment. They had no doubt that the Christ living within them would any day reappear in the glory of His Second Coming and manifest Himself to all men. To renounce a condemned world, whose sentence was so close to being executed, seemed to many people to be an easy thing.

## Men Like Us

Let us be careful, however, not to look upon the first Christians as men of a different category from ourselves or of an essentially different spirituality. In reality, our brothers of those heroic times resemble us more than we imagine. In one very important respect our situation is very much like theirs. Today, to the extent that the world is de-Christianized and under new forms returns to the old idolatries of the state, of race, and of blood, the authentic Christian is scarcely less isolated than were the first Christians under the empire of the Caesars. Many of the early Christians did not protect themselves any more than we do against the corruption which streamed in on them from all sides. Habit prevents us from being sensitive to the contradictions between the Cross and a world that is still so indomitable so many centuries after the first Christians began to measure their strength against paganism.

For the Christians of heroic times there was no question to resolve other than the one which confronts their brothers today: to persevere in the faith in a world without faith, to remain pure in a society delivered to all manner of covetousness. Paul himself recognized that he could not ask the faithful to cut off all commerce with the impure of the world for, he said: "Otherwise you would have to leave the world." But how, without being contaminated, can we breathe the atmosphere which prevailed then and which still prevails today in the great cities of the world?

The invisible Christ did not intervene in this struggle of His followers any more directly then than He does today, as is shown by Saint Paul's denunciation of abuses. Not only ordinary sins but the worst kind of scandals had disgraced the infant Churches: "It is actually reported that there is immorality among you, and such immorality as is not found even among the Gentiles . . ." Paul was speaking of incest. And he did not think it beside the point to remind them that "neither fornicators, nor idolaters, nor adulterers, nor the effeminate, nor sodomites, nor thieves, nor the covetous, nor drunkards, nor the evil-tongued, nor the greedy will possess the kingdom of God."

Even when the era of persecutions began, Christians were not supermen, all desirous of the supreme sacrifice. The same goes for the ideas we have of those other ages marked by so many martyrs, as well as for what lay people think about cloisters, which they believe to be peopled only with saints. In reality, God remains what He is: He never forces Himself upon anyone; but taking His delight in love, he desires from each one of us the response of liberty. The Polyeuctes* of the second century were always free to turn back. Christ does not force anyone's hand; and the primitive, suffering Church, banished from the empire and always under a terrible threat, knew all the demons which torment us today.

The book of Hermas, known as *The Shepherd of Hermas* and composed in the first half of the second century, furnishes evidence of this fact. Hermas, a Christian of Rome and the brother of Pope Pius I, was greatly preoccupied with the moral reform of that Christian society which, from our point of view, seems resplendent with the blood of martyrs. Undoubtedly the two emperors Trajan and Adrian were less ferocious than other Caesars, but the danger always remained acute for Christians. Apostasy was not rare among them, nor was blasphemy or public denial of their faith. Certain martyrs even hesi-

---

* Another Molière character, implying an opportunist, who is likely to become a turncoat under duress.

tated, weak at the thought of the supreme sacrifice. Many of the faithful, after the enthusiasm
of the first days, succumbed anew to the spirit
of the world, as happens today with many converts. Scandals of the flesh were frequent among
them, as was loss of faith. Easy access to confession and absolution did not exist then. Although Hermas does not agree with those who
deny that pardon can be had for sins after baptism, it is certain that in the second century
serious sins meant something very different from
what they do today.

In the following century, when an edict of
Emperor Diocletian forbade circumcision and the
administration of baptism under the pain of death,
Dionysius of Alexandria reported that defection
was universal: "A great number of persons presented themselves of their own accord . . . Called
by their names and invited to sacrifice they came
forward, most of them pale and trembling . . .
The multitude assembled for this spectacle held
them in ridicule; everyone saw that they were
cowards just as timid before offering sacrifices
as before death. Others, however, showed more
confidence: they ran to the altars, protesting

that they had never been Christians . . ." Some
let themselves be put in prison but they abjured
before the tribunal or were overcome by torture.
It was thus in Carthage, in Rome, and in Alexandria; and the bishop of Smyrna defected, taking with him a great number of his faithful.

Thus for our brothers so close to Christ in
time as for Christians today, everything comes
down to perseverance. Whatever the trials they
underwent, their God was no different from the
God known to souls today and whose silence
and absence distress those who trust too much
in the so-called "sensible" manifestations of grace.
For them as for us, it was a question of not
denying in the hour of darkness what has been
revealed in light. Such, basically, is the ancient
Christian drama. How many young people have
given everything, have bound themselves by sol-
emn vows to a God that (for the rest of their
lives) they could not understand except in the
obscurity of a faith that is deprived of sensible
consolations!

Such has been the manner of the invisible
Christ from the beginning of His work in the
heart of humanity. He is there; He is present in

each Christian life. To a few, in certain moments, His presence is manifested with such force that, for them, to give a whole life of service and love is hardly enough. Then the doors close again: what remains is the road to death, landmarked with obligations, a road through the shadows, without the help of any tenderness, in the midst of a world given over to all manner of pleasure. How many martyrs there are who have not seen the heavens open, as did Stephen! But many, fortunately, are courageous enough to leave the shutters closed, thus resisting the temptation to abandon their Hidden God.

## V

# In Imitation of the Executioners
# of Christ

THE extent to which men have professed
their belief in Christ's humanity ought to
have diminished the reign of human ferocity
in history. Undoubtedly there has been some
change; the Incarnation has in point of fact di-
vided history into two distinct periods. Through
Christ the slave has become the brother of his
master. It is, of course, very consoling to take
this point of view, especially if we set it off, as
we are accustomed to do, against the situation
in various totalitarian regimes: there people become inhuman to the extent that they become
un-Christian. This is very comforting for the
Christian to think about; it is very reassuring.

But we are not looking for comfort or reassurance. What matters is not what, from our point of view, ought to have been, but what has been and what is. We believe that man has a certain dignity because he was created in the image and likeness of the Father; in addition, we believe that he shares in a very singular way in the unfathomable mystery of the God-Man, of the Word of God become one of us. It is undeniable that these beliefs applied first of all and in a special way to slaves and to underprivileged groups. The strikingly rapid propagation of Christianity across the empire, if we are looking for a human reason, was due primarily to this sudden dignity bestowed upon slaves and Jews, in an unexpected elevation from which they benefited. For Christ willed to be one of them, He became one of them, and He will remain one of them until the end of time, until that last judgment when He will become identical with them before heaven and earth: "I was hungry and you gave me to eat; I was in prison and you came to me . . . as long as you did it for one of these, the least of my brethren, you did it for me." He was this prisoner; He was this hungry man. Through all hagiography, ever since there were saints to imitate the Lord, runs the legend of the poor man who knocks on a door in the evening, who is taken in or rejected, and who is Christ.

But it is not really legend that is important for us; it is history. Have men treated each other less cruelly from the day they began to believe in the Incarnate Word? In a recent sermon a well-known Jesuit poked fun at unsophisticated people like me who learn history from the poets. But (with all due respect to the good Father) I also learn history from the memoirs and letters of men who massacre and burn other men alive and who have committed such crimes while professing to believe that Christ too was a man.

This is the question: has the Christian Era been marked by respect for man insofar as he has a suffering body capable of enduring much affliction, has a spirit that can be manipulated, has a conscience that can be broken down by torturing the body? Simone Weil was obsessed all her life by the millions of slaves who were crucified before Christ was born, by the immense forest of gibbets upon which so many precursors were nailed and to whom no centurion rendered homage after having heard their last cry. For my part, I am much more obsessed by all the crosses that have been constantly erected after Christ—erected by a blind and deaf Christianity which never recognizes in the poor bodies it submits to questioning the Christ whose pierced hands and feet Christians kiss so piously on Good Friday.

Why has this identity, which the Lord Himself established in terms which none can challenge, been grasped only by the saints or by those striving for sanctity? Certainly *they* are numerous; but why has this fact not been understood by Christian peoples? To take only one example: Spain conquered the New World as a messenger of Christ and in order to evangelize it. Why then did she annihilate many peoples with the worst kind of ferocity: the kind inspired by motives of financial gain? Why does the history of the conquistadors not shock us more? And if I speak of Spain I am not forgetting the beam that is in my own eye as a Frenchman. Nor am I forgetting the good that has been accomplished by us, even without taking into account the work of the missionaries: lands cultivated, mines developed, harbors, roads, and railroads constructed, and, above all, hospitals, dispensaries, and schools. But these works have raised up generations of people who are just as wicked as we are and with whom we have persisted, and still persist, in making enemies.

Industrialization created the proletariat: two horrible words to express two horrible things which have been a source of misery that is greater, perhaps, than that which our missionaries, teachers, and doctors have endeavored to suppress.

*Christ was a man.* Why has this fact had so few consequences and why has it not at all changed the behavior of baptized men? There runs through Christian history, for all kinds of reasons, an attitude of invincible scorn toward less developed peoples. The historical relationship between dominating and dominated peoples has not changed appreciably since the time of Christ, even though, in the economic order, it has not worsened; this has happened to the extent that an increase of power brought to men by Christian liberation has been used to dominate those who did not receive the light. The natural riches

114

of underdeveloped countries has, without their willing it, released a covetousness among Christian nations: a vice which, in attempting to glut itself, has spilled much blood. Their domination is perpetuated by methods which testify that it is not the imitation of Jesus Christ but the imitation of His executioners that has too often been the rule of the Christian West in the course of history.

It would be an illusion to believe that this secular evil is a sickness that we have recently acquired. It would be an illusion to believe that Nazism poisoned the peoples it subjugated and that, if torture is practically re-established among us, we must see in this misfortune a sequel to the Occupation or maintain that the Gestapo contaminated its victims. As a matter of fact, what was more or less clandestine before has now become a normal part of police methods. This is the truth and we can find a parallel in pornography: what was formerly sold under the counter is now available on every newsstand. Similarly, we torture people overtly today.

Undoubtedly it is true that the Gestapo, in the footsteps of the Soviet Secret Police, perfected the art of making men suffer. Electricity applied to certain parts of the human body gives results which could not have been obtained by a more expensive and complicated instrument in the days of Louis XVI. It is astounding what results can be effected with a simple bathtub, or with still less: a lighted cigarette, in certain cases, has worked marvels. Pilate did not intend the scourging, the crowning with thorns, or the mantle of derision as a means of extorting confessions; he merely wanted to give this man who called Himself the Son of God so miserable an appearance that perhaps the crowd and even His enemies themselves would take pity on Him. Today, when we tie a man to a post in a police station—I say "we" because we live in a democracy and we are jointly responsible for these things—we have no desire to take pity on anyone.

Of course, none of this is done without reason or excuses or sometimes without justification. We are the victims of a terribly complicated social system. But whatever our reasons or excuses after nineteen centuries of Christianity, Christ never appears to modern executioners to be one with the criminal; the Holy Face never reveals itself in the countenance of the Arab which is forced to bear the marks of a commissioner's fist. How strange it is that they never think of their God tied to a column and delivered to the cohort, especially when it is a case of one of those dark faces with Semitic features; that they never hear His voice in the cries and supplications of their victim: "You do it to me." One day His voice will be heard, and it will no longer be suppliant. It will cry out to them and to all of us who have accepted and perhaps approved these things: "I was that young man who loved his country and fought for his king; I was that brother whom you forced to betray his brother." Why has this grace never been given to any baptized executioner? Why don't the soldiers of the modern cohort sometimes drop their whips and fall on their knees at the feet of the one they scourge?

When in history have Christian nations ever testified that they remembered that Christ was a man tortured in His body? They cannot be excused because in every age there has been a Vincent de Paul or a Francis of Assisi to remind them of it—not so much by their words as by their lives of sacrifice. But the course of history has not been influenced by the saints. They have acted upon hearts and souls; but history has remained criminal.

Even slavery has never disappeared. The Negroes of America are terribly tragic witnesses to that slave trade which enriched many good people in the old days, whether they were natives of St. Malo, of Bordeaux, or of Nantes. It is not very comforting to have been born in a port city and perhaps to have had ancestors who sailed in armed boats because neither ivory nor spices were their most valuable cargo. I strongly believe that Chateaubriand's father owed a part of his fortune to this trade. Indeed, slave trade is one of those things that is responsible for many great fortunes; it makes us shudder to think of this fact.

Let us consider more closely this man who was called Christ. Who was He? We are not speaking of an abstract man: of man in himself, free from all ethnic considerations. The Son of Man emerged in His beauty, in His mildness, and in His strength from a very obscure background. He was a man among men at a precise moment in history and belonged to a definite society. He could have been rich or poor; He chose to be poor. He could have belonged to a race of lords, the lords of His time: the Romans. He chose to be born a Jew and to be a Jewish worker. How have Christian generations reacted to these two characteristics of the human personality of Christ?

I am sometimes terrified by the thought that all my piety—the piety that I was taught in the school where I made my first fervent Communion, the piety which my mother practiced in our provincial home scented with the odor of good cooking and shaded by towering trees—that all this fervor, that all this love were directed toward a Christ refashioned in my own image and my own likeness, in the image and likeness of my social milieu. My image of Christ was as far removed from His reality as I myself was from the dockworker I hesitated to sit beside in the trolley car, or from one of those Jews working in the open market place in Bordeaux whom I liked to make angry when I was a schoolboy, whom I would tease with the corner of my scarf folded in the form of a pig's ear.

Not that I believe it is necessary to see in the risen Christ only the worker that He was and to interpret everything strictly from that point of view, as there is sometimes a tendency to do today. If there is one truth that stands out in the Gospel, it is that the Lord made no distinction of persons. If Zacchaeus in his sycamore tree had been called Rothschild, He would just as well have said to him: "Rothschild, this day I must abide in thy house." We cannot be sure that a mechanic or a sewerman as such is not more precious in God's eyes than an ambassador, a scholar, or a member of an exclusive club. The Son of Man could just as well have called a policeman and the policeman would have followed Him. Both before and after the Passion Christ found a centurion whom He redeemed and made resplendent by His grace: the one taught us how we must receive the Lord when He comes within us, whispered the words we must say at that moment, and taught us the gesture of striking our breast; and the other centurion, whose prejudices were suddenly shattered by that last great mysterious cry, received the grace to recognize the Savior of the world, the

Son of God, in the criminal covered with spittle, blood, and pus. Centurion or tax collector or doctor of the law—Christ makes no distinction of persons and if the working class has a certain preference, it must not be deified. Nevertheless Christ was a worker and a poor man. *What has been the place of workers, what is their place today in Christian society?*

And Christ was also a Jew. Many reasons have conspired to bring about the anti-Semitism of Christian nations, especially among Catholics; the profound hatred is strengthened in this case by all the excuses which history furnishes. Whatever be these excuses and these reasons, the fact that Christ was a Jewish child, a Jewish boy, a Jewish man, and that His mother resembled a little Jewish girl we perhaps know—none of this has weighed sufficiently in the balance to offset a hatred which has grown stronger from century to century, ending in the crematories of our own day, crematories which are the hideous outcome of centuries of hatred. *Jewish children whom my wife saw at the station in Austerlitz one dark morning during the Occupation, piled in delivery trucks and guarded by French police-*

*men: you will remain forever present in my*
*heart and in my thought!*

Because bitterness and disgust overcome us
here, let us dwell on another lesson suggested
by the fact that Christ was a man. Contempt is
a terrible temptation when one has lived a long
time; I have seen too much of it. There is de-
cidedly nothing to expect, we think in such moments, from this crafty, spiteful, and, above all,
greedy creature who seeks nothing but his own
interest and the enjoyment of wealth acquired
sometimes through the exploitation of a whole
class and the poisoning of a whole people. There
is nothing to be done, we repeat to ourselves,
with this hypocritical creature who disguises his
vilest passions under lofty names and sentiments,
under the name of nationalism in particular. This
is the explanation of totalitarian regimes: all
tyrannies are founded upon contempt for man.
When this temptation to contempt overcomes us,
we must remember that Christ was a man like
us and that He loved us. If He was one of us,
then every man, no matter how miserable he
be, has a capacity for God. Since the Lord belonged carnally to the human race, we must not

despair of a humanity sanctified and glorified by Him; if He loved us, it is because in spite of so many crimes we are worthy of being loved.

Christ did not love men less after His crucifixion than He loved them before He suffered at their hands. On the contrary, the risen Christ showed more tenderness and more love toward His friends than He did before His passion. The harsh words against a race of vipers, against the hypocritical doctors, those words which cursed Capharnaum, Corozain, and Bethsaida did not come from the lips of the stranger who accompanied the two sorrowful men on the road to Emmaus one evening. *And behold a fire was kindled in them while He spoke*—a fire that they would communicate to others and which would never be extinguished! This Christ emerged alive from a hell of suffering. He survived all the tortures that the executioners of all time have inflicted and still inflict with more cowardice than ferocity if possible—for the victim is always bound, always without defense, always like a lamb led to the slaughter—and yet He is there walking beside Cleophas and his companion explaining the Scriptures with the same patience of a pastor or a curate in the suburbs explaining the catechism to two children at the end of a hard day. He whose voice was recognized by an accent of unspeakable tenderness, when He said "Mary!" to the holy woman who sought Him, had survived the tomb; but he also survived the derision and the ignominy of outrages. He showed His wounds to Thomas, not to make him ashamed of belonging to a race of assassins, but in order that he place his fingers in them and, beyond the hole opened by the lance, feel the heartbeat; in order finally to elicit from this unbeliever the cry of adoration that generations of faithful have handed on to us: "My Lord and my God!"

Let us never succumb to the temptation of despising a people whose flesh the Son of Man not only took on and whose nature He assumed, but which He also consecrated with His love. And if we have no right to succumb to the temptation of despising others, neither do we have the right to despise ourselves.

True, we must be horrified when we know ourselves, as Bossuet said. But there is nevertheless a risk here for many souls, for the worst can result from it, provided we understand the worst to be despair. How many young men and women, after having struggled with themselves for a long period of time, finally abandoned a love of which they no longer felt themselves worthy. The education which Catholic children of my generation received exposed them to this danger in a serious way. During retreats we were repeatedly reminded of the words of Blanche de Castille to Saint Louis: "That she would rather see him dead at her feet than guilty of a single mortal sin." The paralytic at our Lord's feet was forcibly burdened with all the sins of a man's poor life. The Lord saw them, held them under His loving gaze; but He asked no questions; He did not become angry. A single sentence sufficed: "Thy sins are forgiven thee."

To say that He who came to seek and save what was lost despises us because of our sins understates the case. He took upon Himself everything in human nature except sin; nevertheless sin remains the bond between Him and us. He came for the prodigal who contemptibly dissipated his patrimony, eating and drinking with prostitutes; for the woman taken in adultery, and for the courtesan. I will not dare say that this is what He loves in us; for it is our repentance He loves and He hates sin. But it is because of sin that He has come, and it is often by this secret wound, by this crevice in the hidden depths of our being, that He makes His way into our poor hearts.

One might say that even our impotence to debase ourselves brings out the incomparable grandeur of the human soul in His eyes. I believe that in addition to compassion there is a sentiment resembling respect in the words spoken to the woman taken in adultery: "Neither will I condemn thee"—as if His divine wisdom discerned an impalpable germ of eternal love in the worst attachments. And how gently He spoke to the sinner of Samaria who must have been held in ill repute among her people, who was perhaps shunned by virtuous women. No, we will not succumb to the temptation of despising ourselves. We will never believe that there can no longer be forgiveness for us. This flesh which we are sometimes so ashamed of and which constantly humiliates us makes each one of us, nevertheless, a brother of Christ.

# THE EXECUTIONERS OF CHRIST

Christ was a man; but He still is; He is always a man. He is always someone living, whose face we know, to whom we speak, and who speaks to us. The union of the least of Christians, if he be in the state of grace, with the Word Incarnate is a union beyond all commentary. I am not speaking here of the contemplation of saints, but of that daily familiarity which is certainly not without danger—without all the risks of habit from sentimentality to false piety. It makes no difference. We are so accustomed to it that we have to talk with our Islamic friends to understand what the solitude of a believer, outside the Incarnation, before infinite Being, and what faith in a God who is our brother, in a man who is our God, means in our life.

This is a wonder that has no explanation: there are as many incommunicable secrets which cannot be captured in words as there are fervent Christians in the world. I exclude saints whose vocation it is to be manifested, usually in spite of themselves, before the eyes of men; ordinary Christians remain silent and die with their secret. Not always, however. The Lord sometimes wills that one of the innumerable dialogues He holds with faithful souls should be known. Such was the case with Blaise Pascal. On November 23, 1649, from about 10:30 in the evening until after midnight, Pascal saw or felt a fire burning within him and at the same time he knew certainty, peace, total and sweet renunciation, and the tears of joy.

Pascal had written the document which records this experience for his own use. If a servant had not found it in the lining of his doublet after his death, we would never have known what grace visited one of the greatest men who ever lived, a man who through humiliations learned to abandon himself to inspirations. Pascal helps us understand what it means to say that Christ, too, was a man, that His agony still endures, and that we must not sleep while the Son of Man watches and suffers. Vigils, sleep, agony, death —God shares all of these states of the human condition with us because He was also a man, but a man present everywhere because He was God. He is present first of all in the Church; He is present by His grace within us as He is present in the Sacrament of the Altar; He is present wherever two or three are gathered together in His name as He is present in each one of our brothers. There is no encounter in which we do not encounter Him; no solitude in which He does not join us; no silence where His voice is not heard deepening, rather than troubling, that silence.

What a grace! But a grace we do not have the right to keep for ourselves. Let us not be like Nicodemus who conversed with the Lord only in the secret of the night. Our hidden life with Christ ought to have some bearing on our lives as citizens. We cannot approve or practice publicly in the name of Caesar what the Lord condemns, disapproves, or curses—whether it be failure to honor our word, exploitation of the poor, police torture, or regimes of terror. If, according to the promise made to us on the Mount, we had been meek, we would have possessed the land.

# The Presence of the Son of Man
# in the Priest

"I AM present to you by my word in Scripture, by my spirit in the Church, by my
inspirations and by *my power in priests* . . ."
These words which Pascal puts in the mouth of
Christ throw light upon one of the aspects of
the Lord's presence among us. His power in
priests: this is a fact which has created misunder-
standings, led to abuses of power, and, worse than
anything, to sacrileges both hidden and visible.
Yet, within the darkness of sinful humanity, the
priesthood still maintains that power to forgive
sins which revealed the Son of God in the Son
of Man. The priest is a stumbling block for
many rebellious spirits; the sacerdotal cast is in-
vested with a spiritual power which, many times

in the course of history, has been badly used to achieve temporal power; priestly power is, nevertheless, a visible sign of the living Christ among us.

The instrument in this case can be none other than ourselves: the Creator has only the creatures at His disposal. Ordinary men like all others, priests are identified with Christ when they raise their hand over a sinner who confesses his sins and asks for grace; or when they take bread in their "holy and venerable" hands; or when, elevating the chalice of the new testament, they re-enact the unfathomable sacrifice of the Lord Himself. Yes, men like all others, but called more than others to sanctity: they are condemned to sanctity in spite of themselves. That many fall by the wayside is a scandal the Church has suffered from the very beginning. That a greater number, although they sometimes weaken, remain faithful and do not dishonor the power confided to them is a miracle to which we have grown so accustomed that we no longer even see it. And yet what a miracle it is that the priesthood has gone on uninterrupted throughout the ages! This is especially true in our own age which flouts chastity and which by every technical means—the press, movies, radio, and television—incites the human animal to satisfaction at every hour of the day and night.

This is the weakness of the Catholic Church; it is the chink in her armor where she has always appeared most vulnerable. Even the storytellers of the ages of faith made fun of the priest and the monk. Nevertheless the sign of the true Church, in which Christ's words remain living, shines forth in this affliction. "Heaven and earth will pass away but my words will not pass away." Here it is not merely a matter of the duration of these words in the memory of men, but of their action, of their power. Priests continue to act, to be efficacious, to consecrate the body of Christ, to forgive sins not through magic of any kind but because the living Christ forgives them. They are, in brief, "spirit and life."

The humanity of most priests overlays the Christ in them, concedes Him to the point that He is in them but as if He were buried. The least "spiritual" of men is identified with the Lord, becomes the Lord, as soon as he whispers the words of absolution or consecration. But when the priest is what is known as "a holy priest," then the Lord is manifested visibly. Christ is suddenly there.

When the time used to come for me to leave on vacation, my humble spiritual director would say to me: "I want to bless you . . ." This sign alone would put me in the presence of the Son of Man, even though I had done nothing but bow my head. I could have put my fingers in the wounds of His side and hands if this priest had, like so many others since Saint Paul, borne the marks of Christ's passion in his flesh. But such a contact would have served only to make more perceptible to me a presence that was already beyond doubt.

In Christian countries and in the ages of faith, there has always been a danger in priestly power. Just as Caesar is tempted to use his power to dominate the people, so Peter has been tempted to use his power to dominate Caesar: this has in fact been our history for two thousand years. The duel of the Priesthood and the Empire has always involved a complicity. Shall we be scandalized by this? We must remember that grace builds on human nature; it does not change it. The will to power inherent in human nature makes use of everything, and even of Christ who is in some sense a victim of it. It was necessary that it be so in spite of all the risks. It was necessary that the words "thy sins are forgiven thee" be pronounced as many times as a sinner expressed his repentance to a man who represented Christ. In this way Christ has become a prisoner of His own creature.

All priests should be saints. And we need a great number of priests: this is a contradiction from which the visible Church tries to free herself in the uncertain combat between grace and nature in the priesthood, and one which will endure until the end of time.

I will pass over what I could say on this subject because I prefer to describe a holy priest I learned of in a recent biography. He was an exceptional priest, of course, for sanctity is always exceptional, even among the consecrated. Yet he reminds me of others I have known. Father Huvelin, the simple curate of St. Augustine's, has innumerable brothers who resemble him. He converted and directed Charles de Foucauld; with that, his fame in future ages would be assured.

He is an unknown saint hidden in the shadow of a celebrated saint; but their destinies, in time and in eternity, are identical.

Charles de Foucauld, at a certain moment in his life, met a priest. It all began one October morning in 1886 in the confessional of St. Augustine's church in Paris. Nothing more common than this encounter between a confessor and a penitent? Rather nothing so strange. Let us listen to the conversation between the Viscount de Foucauld, who remained standing, and the shadow behind the grille:

"Father, I have no faith. I have come to ask you to instruct me."

"Kneel down, make your confession, and you will believe."

"But I didn't come for that."

"Make your confession."

Who was this priest to react so impetuously before an unbeliever? As far as reason is concerned, and even grace, no one would have approved his attitude; the sinner might justifiably have been annoyed and gone away. But the man knelt down and in a few minutes unburdened all the sins he had committed in the course of his prodigal youth. And then, his confession over, he believed.

The priest, a simple curate named Father Huvelin, went further with this still more unexpected command: "Are you fasting? Go to Communion." What! Without preparation! Charles de Foucauld arose; this Communion would be the first of the saint he was to become. If we consider the destiny which was determined in that place and in that hour, we must admit that the curate of St. Augustine's saw beyond all appearances what kind of soul had come to him. The gift of clairvoyance exists; a few have it. On the other hand, perhaps without seeing anything, Father Huvelin obeyed an inspiration which was given to him.

Who was this priest? One of those, it seems, whom humility holds in dread of future glorifications. They cover their tracks; they give themselves, they suffer, and they die. Souls have lived by what they did, said, or wrote; but nothing remains, not even enough to sustain a biography. Father Huvelin belonged to this obscure category, and memory of him would have perished had not Father de Foucauld drawn him in his wake. He will be forever linked with his penitent of October 1886, who himself exclaimed eleven years later, in a meditation dated at Nazareth: "My God, you placed me under the wings of a saint and I remained there. You took me by his hands." As long as Abbé Huvelin lived, Charles de Foucauld remained in his shadow; but thereafter Abbé Huvelin would live in the shadow of the glorified Father de Foucauld.

The October morning of 1886 when he did violence to a soul discloses the essential trait of his nature, or rather the singular character of his vocation, which was expressed later in this remark: "I cannot look at anyone without wanting to give absolution." To my mind these are the most beautiful words ever spoken by a priest, and the truest, too, because they identify him most closely with his Master. The words of the Mass—"This is my body delivered to you, Do this in commemoration of me"—were said only once and in very singular circumstances. But in how many encounters—before creatures carried on stretchers or prostrate in adoration—must the Lord have said: "Thy sins are forgiven thee"?

He came to seek out and to save what was lost. It is for this that each priest, too, is destined. Father Huvelin, who could not look at anyone without wanting to absolve him, fixed the very eye of Christ upon everyone he saw.

But we must understand the meaning of this superhuman desire. There can be no question here of a habit; nor was it merely a painless gesture. The narrative of Father Huvelin's life testifies that, for him, to hear a person's confession was literally to take responsibility for him; it was to take upon himself the destiny of another. The priest who cannot see anyone without wanting to absolve him does so at the price of his crucified life.

The young Huvelin had already proved that he was self-sacrificing when he was still at school. In appearance he was just as pleasant and just as lively as anyone else. Suddenly, however, he surprised the young ogres who surrounded him; he deprived himself of food to an extent that his friends began to worry about him and reported him to the director of the school. But we understand this mortification; the young man had chosen to mortify himself for the sake of others. He had begun to assume responsibility for all that generations of sinners would unburden in the confessional of St. Augustine's.

Very soon suffering overcame him (his body was already deformed by gout). But he never interrupted his work as a preacher and as a confessor. The young man whose fasting at school had frightened his friends became the sick priest who (to fool the servant) turned down the sheets of his bed and rumpled the pillows but spent the nights stretched out on the floor. Assisted by the sacristan, he would ascend the pulpit, even though he was overcome with fatigue and at first unable to speak; then all of a sudden his voice would rise and fill the church. And what did he say? This for example: "Can one make reparation without suffering? Are our Lord's preaching and His words the price of souls? No. We too must suffer to attract a soul and to give it to God." One day he spoke these words which say a good deal for his courage: "The spiritual director must undergo, not in the form of temptation but of experience, what he must protect others from." In this light we can understand what one of his penitents meant: "I know he

saved many people because he succeeded in show-
ing them the reality of evil that was present in
the sins they confessed."

"I cannot look at anyone without wanting to
give absolution." How far did the folly of this
desire carry Father Huvelin? Perhaps he did not
convert Littré (who indeed has ever converted
anyone?); but he was constantly by the old posi-
tivist's side during his last months and he led
him, just before his last breath, to that famous
baptism which caused so much controversy. It
seems quite probable that the last conversations
between Littré and Father Huvelin were but one
long confession. Did the priest resist the temptation to absolve his illustrious penitent who was
not as yet baptized? It is at least arguable, in my
opinion, that he did, just as six years later he ab-
solved Charles de Foucauld, who to all appearances was still an unbeliever.

Love is rash. We can see Father Huvelin in
pursuit of the well-known ex-priest, Hyacinthe
Loyson—the same Hyacinthe Loyson who was
at the origin of the partial disgrace of the beloved Father Mugnier. Could it be said that Father
Huvelin failed in this case? On June 14, 1908,

Hyacinthe Loyson wrote to him: "When the hour comes, you will be notified by my relatives. Then kneel down, wherever you are and say from the bottom of your loving and believing heart the beautiful prayer of the Church: *proficiscere, anima christiana!*" Such were the failures of Father Huvelin.

While Father de Foucauld pursued from one monastery to another—from Nazareth to Béni-Abbès to Tamanrasset—the martyrdom which he greatly desired, his director lived an obscure life in the church of St. Augustine, dragging his suffering body from the altar to the pulpit, from the pulpit to the confessional. Then one day, on June 10, 1910, upon returning from the confessional, he fell to the ground, dying. His agony was silent; yet he murmured three words: "*amabo nunquam satis*" (I will never love enough).

If Bernanos were alive we could hope that he would take the themes found in this life and wed them to the fulgurating intuitions which he, a layman, had of what a saintly priest was—as though he carried within him the living germ of such sanctity, as if the characters invented by the novelist gave birth to a consecrated creature within him. He lived like a man who is nowhere at home, and perhaps he jeered at us in his writings only because he did not have Father Huvelin's priestly power to forgive us.

The power of the priest stands out in the curate of St. Augustine's: not "the power and the glory," but the power and the opprobrium.

# Epilogue: The Final Answer

IF I WERE to give a human reason for my
fidelity to Christ in this evening of my life,
I would call it His quieting of the radical anguish that is in me. This anguish is not to be
confused with the fear spoken of by Lucretius,
that gives birth to gods. For anguish is not fear.
My very singular anguish, which I did not learn
from anyone, tormented me from the moment I
began to grow aware of the tragedy implied in
the fact of being a man; that is to say, a creature
condemned to death and who lives under a stay
of execution for an unknown length of time.
This stay grows shorter each year and my life
resembles that "sorrowful flesh" which one of
Balzac's heroes contemplated with horror as it

shrank to the size of a coin in his trembling hand.

Anguish is so consubstantial to the human condition that is already cruelly manifest in childhood. I still remember, to the point of reliving them, those early torments in my unlighted bedroom; I still hear those slow and heavy footsteps on the stairway; and I still bury my head beneath the blankets. I still feel the hot tears that coursed down my cheeks when, as a boarding-school student, I watched the flickering gas flame trace vacillating shadows on the walls of the dormitory. Perhaps I was a small, timid boy who felt himself less robust than the others in the playground filled with noise and quarrels. Perhaps I was afraid of being called to the head of the room by a contemptuous teacher who was quite capable of making me appear ridiculous and idiotic before my classmates. Perhaps, too, I remember the room in my parents' home where someone had died some time before and where the shutters remained forever closed upon a horrible mystery. Each object in it seemed to have suffered death's somber magic: the glass of water, the arrested pendulum, the armchair still sagging near the fireplace where the fire would never again be lighted.

Yes, for many children anguish is a secret and permanent state. To keep from going insane, I needed the limitless love which my mother poured out on me, the touch of her hand upon my brow during those terrible nights, the comfort of her breath in my hair, and the sound of her voice softly complaining: "What's the matter, silly child? What are you afraid of? I am here; close your eyes and go to sleep."

What, indeed, was tormenting me? My memories help me acknowledge this fact: anguish does not come from without; it is in no way linked to the catastrophes of a given age. The anguished child that I was lived in a time when the war we were fighting concerned only King Behanzin and when the refrain which a blind man chanted in the courtyard of our home reminded me that the French flag had just been raised at Madagascar. There was much argument about us apropos of a certain Dreyfus but his misfortunes did not sadden me at all. In fact, almost all the famous people (people who would not have harmed a fly) had only one fear: that Dreyfus would not be convicted again.

My anguish of later years already existed in that child of a comfortable family in the third Republic—bourgeois, powerful, rich, peaceful, although capable of aggression for a good cause.

Of course, I do not pretend that the era of calamities which began in 1914 (the first premonitions of which were evident much earlier) has not nourished the anguish of modern man or that there was no causal relationship between the unhappiness of the times and the existential anguish of "being in the world." But these events, however tragic they were, did not create my anguish, even though they obliged me to relate it to the vissicitudes of history. Let us say that we can no longer "distract" ourselves from them, in accordance with Pascal's use of that word. I believe that even in those ages when history confronted human nature with nothing that was singularly tragic, in the peaceful and happy ages —peaceful and happy at least for the privileged classes, because there is never a happy age for the working class—man was smitten by the unhappiness that comes of being a man who loves and is not loved; who is loved and does not love; who had a son and lost him; who was young and is so no longer; who was strong and healthy and who one day heard a doctor tell him, after a long examination, "We might try an operation . . . ," and who hears the automobiles in the streets, a radio playing upstairs, a woman's laughter, but who knows that in six months he will be dead. But even if this trial is spared him there remains the adequate torture (as Michelet called old age) of the gradual deterioration of strength, the decline of the mind, the slow and noiseless approach of ineluctable dissolution.

In this matter I disagree with Michelet and so many others and I exclaim with Lacordaire: "Gentlemen, I bring you happiness." I bring you the kind of happiness that a Christian begins to discover at my age. In the measure that I have grown old, anguish has loosened its grip on me. "The man who grows old becomes more aware of the eternal," says Romano Guardini. "He is less agitated and the voices from beyond are better heard. The encroachment of eternity pales the reality of time." There is a prayer by Saint Gertrude, who must have been very old when she uttered it, in which she calls Christ "the love of the evening of my life" and in which she says: "O my Jesus of life's evening, let me fall asleep in you quietly. . . ." But all of this was already expressed at the dawn of the Christian Era when the aged Simeon pressed the infant God to his breast: *Nunc dimittis servum tuum, Domine* . . .

Christ is not a defense which I have erected against anguish; on the contrary, anguish was a permanent state during the days of my stormy youth when I did not have recourse to Him, when I dealt apart from Him. No, my anguish did not create God. The quieting I now experience, the silence that falls upon my last days, permits me finally to be attentive to the answer which was unceasingly given during my tormented life, but to which I preferred my suffering because I preferred my sin. What more do I know today than I did as a despairing adolescent? The adolescent loves neither happiness nor peace. It took me a long time to learn to love God. I can say nothing on this subject that is not part of my life: as an adolescent I loved my anguish and I preferred it to God. Far from inciting me to imagine a God to deliver me, my anguish provided me with reasons and excuses to escape the presence, in me and about me, of a love to which I preferred an unhappiness born of covetousness.

It is not anguish which creates the Father in heaven whom Christ taught us to know and to love. It was rather my anguish, the somber delectation that lasted throughout my interminable youth—I say interminable because my heart remains young even though I am not—it was this delectation in anguish that inclined me to turn away from God and even deny that He existed. It furnished me with arguments and proofs against His goodness, against His love.

This is undoubtedly not true of all men. But it is true of those writers and poets who cherish in their anguish the very source of their inspiration, and more precisely in that form of anguish which is born of an attraction for a God who is rejected by flesh and blood. I have often applied to myself the image from Maurice de Guérin in which he compared his thought to a heavenly fire that burns on a horizon between two worlds.

It is the torture of being incapable of choosing between the world and God that constitutes in effect the drama of many artists—a drama which both torments and delights them.

"If thou didst know the gift of God," Christ said to the Samaritan woman. And what is the gift of God? It is precisely the opposite of anguish. "Peace I leave with you; my peace I give to you," Christ repeated to His friends on the last night, before He entered into His agony. It is precisely this peace which we do not want; it appears redoutable to us because we do not love peace. "Arise, desired tempests!" was the cry of René at the dawn of the Romantic Age; and this cry reveals the vocation of so many young people to unhappiness. I went first of all to the damned poets and they attracted me to the prince of darkness and his eternal unhappiness. Was this literature? Yes, but it was a strange literature in which despair was so often, in surrealist circles, authenticated by suicide. Saint John denounces this hatred of peace; he tells us that light came into the world and that men refused it because they preferred darkness. The creature seeks darkness to obliterate himself. The victory of Christ in a life is summed up in this difficult acceptance of peace in light.

I am aware of this objection: Christianity itself is anguish. But it is not enough to say that there is a Christian anguish. All those who revolted against Christianity in the nineteenth century accused it of being against nature, of having darkened the world, of having calumniated life. It is true that the name of Christianity masks many contradictory tendencies which set Christians at odds with one another. Those who are called to love one another have burned each other. There are many mansions in the Father's house. And one of them, from Saint Augustine through Calvin and Jansen, was erected under the sign of fear and trembling: anguish in the strictest sense of the word. But there is another anguish which is less harsh: that of love which is totally contained in the regret of having offended the loved one, in the fear of no longer being loved by him, and of no longer feeling ourselves capable of loving him. The love of the creature for the Creator is no more exempt from what Marcel Proust calls the intermittences of the heart than human love. But this is not the anguish we refer to when we speak of fear and trembling.

Monsieur de Saint-Cyran has always seemed to me to be the worst kind of theologian. Let us say that in France, to speak only of France, Port-Royal is still the most illustrious source of that anguish which is centered upon an obsession with personal salvation. The Infinite Being refuses or gives His grace according to an unpredictable plan to a creature tainted from birth, totally impotent except to do evil (for in what concerns evil, human nature has the power of a god). We are delivered naked, trembling, disarmed, to an arbitrary God. This is the root of Jansenist anguish.

It is impossible to indicate in a few words the contents of the immense work in which, over the centuries, a whole school of Christian thinkers have collaborated. I will simply allude to the permanent source of anguish and even of despair that a certain theology has premised upon a wounded heart. It has generated innumerable and lamentable progeny, the terror of Catholic confessors: those scrupulous souls obsessed by trifles, adorers of a niggling divinity with whom we must bargain craftily. André Gide denounced

Catholics for their "cramp of salvation." This cramp is so painful that many young people who began by following Christ drew away from Him to escape the frightful obligation of rendering an account of their least desire, their least thought. They threw the whole Christian heritage overboard. "What is wonderful about Communism," a recent convert to Marxism told me one day, "is that my personal salvation no longer interests me."

What I propose as a defense against this form of anguish is another anguish which is generative of peace and joy. I propose a kind of spiritual homeopathy, that is, a release from anguish through anguish. Obsession with our personal salvation will not be dominated and conquered in us unless it is transposed to the order of charity. It goes without saying that we should nourish the hope of salvation and that the whole of a Christian life ought to tend toward eternal life. But if it is clear that we ought to have a passionate desire for salvation, we should not be obsessed with it in the pathological sense of the word. In my youth I was frequently seduced by the words which Pascal put in Christ's mouth: "I thought of you in my agony. I lost so much blood for you." These words impress me less today because I discern in such a desire for redemptive blood the complacency of a creature resigned to the eternal damnation of most of the human race, and not agonized by the thought that he is set apart with a small flock of the elect.

Anguish transmuted into charity, *anguish for another*, delivers us from the terror felt by so many Christian souls before the mystery of predestination and liberates us from an obsession with personal salvation, not in respect to what is essential but in respect to what is morbid. Our anguish then becomes more than a matter of personal concern: it embraces mankind or, at least, that part of mankind which is "the neighbor" for us and can extend to a social class or to entire peoples. For a worker priest, the neighbor is the whole working class, as the Jews were for us during the Nazi persecution.

For Sartre "hell is other people"; but for us, others are Christ. He tells us Himself that the Son of Man is come to save what is lost, *all* that is lost and not merely this one or that one for whom He would have consecrated a special, miserly drop of His blood.

The Christian life is first of all a personal relationship between each one of us and God. "You have not chosen me; I have chosen you." It goes without saying that the extension of our anguish to embrace the suffering of men will not yield all of its fruits unless our apostolate is rooted in a life of close intimacy with Christ. I believe, I have always believed, that the Christian life is essentially a friendship, a love (and therefore that which is most personal, most individual), that each one of us has been called by his name, and that at the beginning of every conversion there is this encounter at the turning of the road spoken of by Lacordaire—an encounter with an adorable being, demanding, tenacious, whom nothing discourages, and to whom we prefer so many creatures whom we shortly forsake or who forsake us. But He is always there, never so close to us as when we believe Him to be absent, awaiting His hour which, in the case of many men, is unfortunately the last, when there is no longer any possibility of betrayal.

155

But what is the reality of this Christ whom all believers strive to imitate, unless it be that He took upon Himself our human anguish? Therefore, we must also take upon ourselves the anguish of each other. The saints did so literally, to the point of identifying themselves with the Father's abandonment of His Son in the horror of the night. This secret of Christ's agony was profoundly understood by Bernanos. And this is what gives his fictional priests, particularly the country priest, their mysterious density. For us, as simple faithful, it is sufficient to unite ourselves with the anguish, experienced by Christ, in our brothers.

Here, then, is the strange remedy for anguish which I propose: peace and joy are the fruits of anguish. "Peace I leave with you, my peace I give to you: not as the world gives do I give to you." We understand now the profound meaning of the last promise which the Son of Man made to us before entering into His agony: peace and joy in this plentitude of suffering which consists in espousing, each one according to his vocation, the suffering of the hungry, the persecuted, the imprisoned, the tortured, the exploited. This is the Christian paradox.

We know that there is a difference between human hope and spiritual hope. We may lose all hope for the temporal salvation of mankind and still await the kingdom of God. In the very midst of the Atomic Age, we await it confidently. But it must not be concluded from this that our hope concerns only eternity; it also concerns the dark world of the living. For the crimes of the will to power which sum up temporal history do not prevent the leaven of which Christ speaks from working tirelessly in the human mass. The fire which He came to cast upon the earth is always smoldering and the bloodiest years of history are nevertheless years of grace.

"Thy kingdom come," we pray in the Our Father. Millions and millions of human beings have prayed thus over the nearly two thousand years since this prayer was taught to us, and with the absolute certitude of being answered. Indeed the prayer is already answered; the kingdom has already come; it is among us, within us in such a way that we are never defeated except in appearance. And as our anguish is the very condition of our peace, our defeat is the very condition of our victory. "Fear not; I have overcome the world." He who challenged the world so boldly did so at the very hour when He was about to be betrayed, outraged, made a laughingstock, nailed to the gibbet of a slave.

Saint Paul tells us that all of creation groans and suffers the pains of childbirth. Our anguish is indeed inspired by childbirth and it seems interminable by our ephemeral standards. But those of us who have kept the faith know what the end will be. To those who succumb to anguish and who are about to lose heart, we can do no better than repeat what Saint Paul affirmed to the faithful of Rome: "Who shall separate us from the love of Christ? Shall tribulation, or distress, or persecution, or hunger, or nakedness, or danger, or the sword? But in all these things we overcome because of him who has loved us."

ABOUT THE AUTHOR

François Mauriac was born at Bordeaux, France, in 1885 and was educated in that city at Roman Catholic schools and at Bordeaux University. "The history of Bordeaux," he says, "is the history of my body and my soul: it is my childhood and my youth crystallized."

Mauriac undertook philosophical studies at the Ecole des Chartes in Paris, but gradually abandoned scholarship for the writing of fiction. *A Kiss for the Leper*, a novel written in 1922, quickly made him famous, and his writings since that time have won him world renown. In 1933 he was elected a member of the French Academy. Shortly afterward, he began his controversial political writing, which he continued during the years of the Resistance under the name Forez, and finally, in 1945, he became a brilliant editorial writer on *Le Figaro*. In 1952, M. Mauriac won the Nobel Prize, a fitting recognition of the original type of novel he has evolved and of his many admirable plays. In 1959, Mauriac was elected an honorary member of the American Academy of Arts and Letters.

*This book was set in*
*Janson types by*
*Slugs Composition Company.*
*It was printed and bound by*
*The Haddon Craftsmen.*
*The typography and design are by*
*Larry Kamp*